York

Issues in Physical Education
for the Primary Years

CONTEMPORARY ANALYSIS IN EDUCATION SERIES
General Editor: Philip Taylor

Contemporary Analysis in Education Series

Issues in Physical Education for the Primary Years

Edited by

Anne Williams

The Falmer Press
(A member of the Taylor & Francis Group)
London · New York · Philadelphia

UK The Falmer Press, Falmer House, Barcombe, Lewes, East Sussex. BN8 5DL

USA The Falmer Press, Taylor & Francis Inc., 242 Cherry Street, Philadelphia, PA 19106–1906

First published 1989

British Library Cataloguing in Publication Data

Issues in physical education for the primary years
1. Primary schools. Curriculum subjects:
Physical education. Teaching
I. Williams, Anne
372.8'6044

ISBN 1-85000-534-6
ISBN 1-85000-535-4 Pbk

Library of Congress Cataloging-in-Publication Data

Issues in physical eduction for the primary years/Anne Williams
p.   cm.
Bibliography: p.
Includes index.
ISBN 1-85000-534-6. — ISBN 1-85000-535-4 (pbk.)
1. Physical education for children — Great Britain.
2. Physical education for children — Great Britain
— Curricula.
I. Williams, Anne.

GV245.I84 1989
372.8'6 — dc 19
89-1222 CIP

Jacket design by Len Williams

Typeset in Great Britain by Morley Harris Typesetting,
36a Cotham Hill, Cotham, Bristol

Contents

List of Tables and Figures

Chapter 1:
Introduction –
The Changing Context of Physical Education

Anne Williams

School physical education gives many children their only opportunity to develop physical potential. Children of primary school age have an interest in, and a thirst for, activity. Physical education in the primary school is thus of crucial importance. It satisfies a need for activity, provides an opportunity for laying the foundations of a lifelong interest in physical activity, and is a medium by which many of the aims of education can be achieved. Its educational potential will of course only be realized if a well-planned, broad and balanced curriculum is offered.

The current high profile of education has resulted in many aspects which have hitherto been seen as the province of the 'professionals' becoming matters of public debate. The increased involvement of central government, of parents, and of local community interests means that the activities which constitute the school day are being critically scrutinized by a much wider audience than has been the case in the past. It is against this background that some of the influences on the primary curriculum are considered in this chapter.

The National Curriculum

The increased involvement of government in educational policy has been a feature of the last decade, culminating in the publication of the 1988 Education Reform Act which includes proposals for a National Curriculum.

Discussion of the extent to which the National Curriculum proposals reflect an acceleration in an already clearly signposted direction rather than a change of course is beyond the scope of this chapter but can be followed up elsewhere (Williams and Jenkins, 1988).

Curriculum documents have consistently included physical education in the 'core', either implicitly, through areas of experience which include the physical, or explicitly as a named subject area. Physical education is now to become a foundation subject for all pupils aged 5–16, since the Education Reform Act prescribes that the basic curriculum should be implemented for all registered pupils of compulsory school age in maintained schools (clause 2). The word 'become' has been used advisedly. We have to ask whether a physical education curriculum is currently provided for ALL pupils, and if not, what are the implications of a movement towards compulsory provision for all.

Quite apart from children with special physical education needs, who are the focus of chapter 8, there are currently a number of schools in which physical education is seen as one subject from which those pupils who have other identified needs may be legitimately removed. In others, withdrawal from the physical education lesson is seen as a useful form of punishment. This is clearly unacceptable. Unfortunately, for many primary school teachers, a slight reduction in class size may well be seen as an advantage which compensates for the disadvantage to the pupils involved.

Provision for all and differentiation demand a quite radical change of emphasis on the part of the teacher. As Meek (1986) says, the physical education curriculum has developed in such a way that,

> the product might have been generally nourishing but little regard was given to individual tastes.

There is little mention of teaching styles in the DES publications, although HMI are frequently critical of the excessive use of didactic methods. In primary schools, teachers who use individualized programmes and ability-related group work in much of their classroom teaching can often be observed teaching physical education using a direct and didactic approach with little or no task differentiation. It is clear that if the starting point is to be, "What can this child do?", rather than, "Can this child do what we are doing?" styles of teaching will, in many cases, need to change. Those of us in mainstream education could learn much from those in special schools on this issue. If we have to offer a diet

2

which is no longer indigestible by some, it may well prove to be enjoyable rather than merely palatable for the majority.

The focus here is on the experience of the individual child. Chapters 4 and 5 discuss aspects of curriculum developments in physical education which encourages a child–focussed approach.

The Community

Emphasis has so far been upon the individual nature of pupils' needs which result from innate or socially determined differences. The range of previous experience which primary pupils bring to physical education has also widened enormously in recent years as a result of increased opportunities within local communities for taking part in leisure time activities and in more serious sport. Recently, there has been unprecedented attention given to the place of sport within physical education and to the role of the teacher in laying the foundations of future sporting performance. It is most important that the primary school teacher recognizes the educational potential and the limitations of sport in the context of the physical education curriculum. Outside the school there are now many more opportunities than ever before for youngsters to participate in sport. The proliferation of boys' football teams is such that good primary age soccer players are frequently playing too many matches as evidenced by increased over-use injuries. Gymnastics clubs now offer opportunities for many youngsters to be challenged and extended. This, of course, does not always make the teacher's task any easier, since the result may well be a group of pupils well ahead of others in the class in terms of their range of skills and movement sophistication.

For those who do not wish to take part in 'serious' sport, there are greatly increased leisure and recreational facilities. In 1971, Emmett found that secondary school leavers' awareness of physical activities was restricted largely to those which they had experienced at school. The picture today is vastly different. Even the 7–year–olds interviewed by the writer spoke of a wide range of physical activities of which they were aware either through the media or through opportunity to try the activities out locally or while on holiday. Physical education curriculum work is therefore taking place in a very different context from that of the 60s and early 70s.

It is also a more varied context, because, while opportunities have widened, access to them is not evenly distributed among the population. Users of leisure and recreation facilities remain predominantly male and middle class, with ease of access and therefore car ownership, a major factor in facilitating sports and leisure centre use.

Informal play activity is also unevenly distributed. White and Coakley (1986) note the tendency for parents to deny girls the opportunities given to boys to play informal games away from the home. This restriction is often because of fears for girls' safety, although also linked to differential social conditioning which operates for boys and girls. It does mean that girls are denied access to an experience of physical activity which many boys are able to enjoy. Different cultures and communities also vary in their commitment to play activity and in their attitude towards giving children the freedom to join in informal play.

Unfortunately, despite increased opportunities available for youngsters wishing to participate in physical activity, most evidence suggests that, generally, primary school children's physical activity levels are much lower than is desirable. Many factors contribute to this: the spread of car ownership; time spent watching TV; unwillingness to allow children to play away from the home because of fears for their safety and so on. The spread of coronary heart disease in Western society has been blamed largely upon the inadequacies of our adult lifestyles. It is only recently that attention has begun to focus upon young children. It is now suggested that potentially harmful fatty deposits can be found in the blood of children of primary school age and that the promotion of an active lifestyle should be targetted not just at the high risk adult population, but also at young children. While activity levels achieved in curriculum time are unlikely to be sufficient to attain or maintain adequate fitness levels physical education must nevertheless be well placed to educate in and about health related fitness. This aspect of the primary school curriculum is discussed in chapter 4.

The Pupil

The pupil is, of course, central to the educational process, and it goes without saying that curriculum experiences should be planned to take account of the child's physiological make-up and consequent response to physical activity, and of the learning process itself including the individual child's learning capacity. These areas are discussed in chapters 6 and 7 respectively.

The principle that all pupils should have equal access to educational opportunities is not new, but has changed in focus with many implications for physical education. The concept of equality of opportunity was first formally recognized in the 1944 Education Act. Early concerns were the underachievement of working class children compared with their middle class peers. Various organizational and methodological initiatives were utilized in order to try to redress the disadvantages of birth, culminating in the reorganization of secondary education from a tripartite to a comprehensive system, thereby abolishing the 11+ examination which had been such a straitjacket in many junior schools. At the same time, the concept of equality of opportunity was being broadened to encompass inequalities based upon race and gender as well as those which were class-based. The Sex Discrimination Act (1975) and the Race Relations Act (1976) gave formal recognition to the rights of all citizens to equality of opportunities in education and in adult life. These laws have, in addition to assisting in preventing overt forms of discrimination, contributed to the general raising of consciousness about more subtle discrimination resulting from often unconscious bias and stereotyping.

After a variety of generally rather simplistic answers to problems of class, race and gender inequalities, it has been recognized that the whole issue is complex and that the effects of class, race and gender are frequently mutually reinforcing. Some aspects of these are the focus of chapters 9 and 10.

A further aspect of the concept of equal opportunity is that concerning children with special educational needs. The report of the Warnock Committee and the 1981 Education Act, both recommending that children with special needs should, as far as is practicable, be educated in mainstream schools, have added a new dimension to the already wide range of developmental, maturational and ability levels faced by the primary school teacher. Not only are teachers being confronted with children whose physical education needs can clearly not be met through that which has hitherto been offered to the mainstream pupils, but the presence of SEN children may well promote a greater awareness of children who have always been in mainstream school, but who have always had special physical education needs. All too often, such children have been left to flounder in the wake of their more able peers. The challenges facing the primary school teacher in this area are discussed in chapter 8.

All of the above highlights the individual nature of pupils' needs. Catering for these requires that careful thought be given to teaching styles and to learning processes. Both have been the focus of considerable attention in recent years. Mosston's work in the USA on a spectrum of teaching styles for physical education has aroused considerable interest among those responsible for training secondary physical education teachers in this country. The emphasis is upon the desirability of having a range of teaching styles at one's disposal. While the ability to vary teaching approaches has been a feature of classroom work in the primary school for some time, this facility has not always been extended to physical education.

Perhaps for understandable reasons, such as concern for pupil safety and organizational difficulties, physical education lessons have tended to remain class, rather than individually, orientated and to feature didactic transmission styles of teaching rather than utilizing problem-solving or discovery learning approaches. Some of the advantages and the difficulties of adopting a child-centred and experiential learning approach to the teaching of games are described in chapter 5.

There is no doubt that a major inhibitor to innovations in primary school physical education teaching is an excessive concern with the product in terms of winning school teams and skilful rather than intelligent and knowledgeable performers. As the Physical Education Association Committee of Enquiry points out, both parents and teachers need to be made aware of the values of physical education.

'Parents need re-educating to ensure that team games are not seen as the only relevant form of physical education'.

A focus upon the individual pupil and an assessment of the curriculum based upon the achievement of all pupils in a range of physical activities could redress the balance.

The Teacher

Despite all the moves to increase accountability and to centralize control of the curriculum, the primary school teacher remains one of the most important influences on the pupils' experience. There has been much criticism of the training given to most primary teachers in physical education. There seems no doubt that trends in both secondary and higher education are likely to leave the teacher less rather than more adequately prepared for physical education curriculum work.

Compared with twenty-five years ago, the difference between the type of programme followed by the 11-year-old and the sixth-former is considerable. Twenty-five years ago certain core activities, gymnastics, athletics, games, dance and possibly swimming were taught to the entire secondary school age range. Flexibility was generally limited to an element of choice within these activities or to the opportunity to opt out of some of them in the senior school.

Today they can only be said to form the basis of the programme in the lower part of the school. As pupils progress through the school, the range of activities open to them is generally extended as is their freedom to withdraw from some or all of the earlier programmes. This tends to lead to emphasis on activities which may be pursued by small groups for reasons of practicality and administrative convenience. By the time pupils reach their last years at school, activities are mainly recreational pursuits, intended to provide a framework upon which adult use of leisure may be based. Programmes are organized in a variety of ways, so that the involvement of the staff tends to become more administrative than teaching. Many schools make no pretence of offering any compulsory programme to senior pupils and many more, while in principle leaving physical education in the curriculum for all pupils, take no action against those who wish to avoid participation and plan their activities on the assumption that a significant number of their pupils will never take part.

The result of this is that activities previously taught to secondary school pupils for between four and seven years, are now being taught for two or three, if at all. Consequently, whereas potential teachers have, in the past, entered college with a background of recent experience in the types of activity which they are shortly to be expected to teach, today they may have only dim memories of such activities, and may not have taken any active interest in sport or recreation immediately prior to embarking on their training. Colleges therefore can no longer assume recent experience in certain activities, as they were able to in the past.

Trends in higher education are unlikely to provide time for the greater help and training that potential teachers need. Early degree courses reduced the time available for professional curriculum work in the quest for academic respectability. The requirement now laid down

7

by the Council for the Accreditation of Teacher Education (CATE) that all BEd courses must include two years of subject study, has not helped those attempting to provide adequate time for courses in the range of curriculum subjects in which primary school teachers are expected to be competent.

One way forward is to strengthen the role of the curriculum leader. This means that responsibility allowances should be given for promoting curriculum work, rather than, as has been the case in the past, for running school teams. However, the allowances available to most schools are such that there is no possibility of every subject having a curriculum leader paid above main professional grade for this job alone. Teachers are thus likely to remain very much dependent upon the quality of the preparation which they receive in initial training and upon subsequent in-service opportunities. This book plays its part in this process by encouraging prospective and practising teachers to reflect upon their work.

References

DES (1977) *Education in Schools: A Consultative Document*, London, HMSO.

DES (1980a) *A Framework for the School Curriculum*, London, HMSO.

DES (1980b) *A View of the Curriculum*, (HMI Series: Matters for Discussion), London, HMSO.

DES (1981) *The School Curriculum*, London, HMSO.

DES (1983) *Curriculum 11–16: Towards a Statement of Entitlement*, London, HMSO.

DES (1984) *The Organization and Content of the 5–16 Curriculum*, London, HMSO.

DES/DOE (1987) *Sport in Schools Seminar*, London, DOE.

EMMETT, I. (1971) *Youth and Leisure in an Urban Sprawl*, Manchester, Manchester University Press.

HOUSE OF COMMONS (1987) *Education Reform Bill*, London, HMSO.

MEEK, C. (1986) 'The contribution of physical education to the new curriculum', *Physical Education Review*, 9, 2.

MURDOCH, E. (1988) *Sport in Schools*, (Desk study commissioned by the DES and DOE) London, Sports Council.

PHYSICAL EDUCATION ASSOCIATION (1987) *Physical Education in Schools, Report of a Commission of Enquiry*, London, PEA.

SCHOOL SPORT FORUM (1988) *Sport in Schools*, London, Sports Council.

WHITE, A. and COAKLEY, J. (1986) *Making Decisions*, London, Sports Council.

WILLIAMS, E.A. and JENKINS, C. (1988) 'Reaction to reform — The National Curriculum proposals and physical education', *Physical Education Review*, 11, 2.

Part A:
The Subject and the Curriculum

Chapter 2:
The Place of Physical Education in Primary Education

Anne Williams

This chapter addresses the question of what we mean by physical education in the context of junior school education. It begins with some observations about the status of physical education as a curriculum subject and then addresses the question of how physical education can contribute to the achievement of the aims of education for the junior school child.

The Status of Physical Education

Physical education has long suffered from a status problem and from confusion about its nature and its relationship with allied activities such as sport and recreation. The existence of a subject hierarchy in which physical education is consistently placed lower rather than higher in the subject pecking order has produced a tendency for physical educationists to be defensive about their subject and to seek to argue for greater recognition of its educational worth. Primary teachers have frequently been prime targets for criticism by those working in physical education, for their failure to appreciate the value of physical education and for their failure to teach the subject 'properly' (PEA, 1987; School Sport Forum, 1988).

It is obvious that the extent to which physical education can be construed as 'educational' depends largely upon the particular definition of education which prevails. One source of the problems faced by physical education in this respect can be traced to the 1960s and 1970s, and, in particular, to the work of a few influential philosophers of education working at that time.

Neither Richard Peters nor Paul Hirst would include physical education as an educational activity according to their own criteria, and neither would John White, discussing the compulsory curriculum. Their denial of physical education's place in the educational process is discussed fully in Kirk (1988). It is perhaps not surprising that physical educationists are defensive about their subject when they see it some- what arbitrarily excluded from the world of education. It is, however, quite obvious that what goes on in school is very much wider ranging than the pursuit of those activities deemed as 'educational' by those such as Peters, Hirst or White. There is certainly little in the National Curriculum documents or in the Education Reform Act to suggest that its proponents have been unduly influenced by these philosophers.

Now it may well be argued that the conceptions of education put forward by the philosophers of the 1960s and 1970s no longer hold great currency, and that the status of educational philosophy as a discipline is now questioned. Nevertheless, the effect on those seeking to establish physical education's educational credentials has only been to produce defensiveness and a plethora of justifications for its curriculum place.

Part of the 'problem' of physical education is that it is seen as a peripheral subject in the curriculum, rather than a central one, and that it is given a status which is inferior to that accorded to the academic pursuits which are seen as central and crucial to the educational process.

The marginal status of physical education is noted by Hargreaves (1977) who sees the subject towards the bottom of a hierarchical order of knowledge which rates 'academic' subjects as superior to 'practical' subjects. Hendry (1976) has drawn attention to the marginal role occupied by the physical education teacher who rarely contributes to discussion of serious educational matters. The tendency within the DES to ignore physical education altogether, or to accord it a couple of sentences also labels the subject as marginal in the eyes of those reading its publications. *The Curriculum 11–16* physical education section was published as an annexe to the main document, alongside other subjects also thereby labelled as marginal.

Further insight into subject status at a theoretical level is offered by Meyer (1980) who categorizes subjects in terms of 'universality' and 'centrality'. Almost all students will follow a number of universal curriculum subjects, that is, subjects where there is general agreement by the public and the profession that enrolment in them is essential for all, or nearly all students of school age. Such subjects would include mathematics, English and physical education. Other subjects, while on the curriculum, would not be seen as universal and would be available only to some students or some groups of students. These subjects probably appear more often at secondary than at junior level and would include classics, music, Russian or economics.

Subjects may also be classified as either central or peripheral. A subject or group of subjects is defined as central if it is seen as essential for students at a particular stage in schooling. Mathematics would be seen by most as both central and universal. Physical education, on the other hand, although universal, would generally be labelled as peripheral, in that, although commonly pursued by almost all pupils it can be omitted from an individual's timetable altogether without that individual being considered to be missing out on a fundamental part of education.

Meyer makes the point that, although teachers are thought to enjoy a certain amount of professional autonomy and therefore choice in what they teach, and this would be particularly true of the junior school teacher, this freedom is actually more apparent than real. He suggests that many other powerful interested parties, which he calls 'legitimating publics' exert a subtle but strong influence on the curriculum, and that subjects and innovations only survive in schools if they enjoy this wider support. An extreme example of this in action is in the affair of the William Tyndale school. Here the failure of the teachers to convince the legitimating publics (initially the parents in this instance) of the educational credibility of their policies, eventually led to the school's closure.

Since mathematics is seen as occupying a central place in the curriculum, significant legitimating publics include employers and those involved in selection for higher education as well as parents. Physical education is of rather less importance to these groups. Discussion about mathematics tends to centre upon the relevant content, the subject's position in the curriculum being generally accepted. Since physical education is not central and since it does not occupy high status, its public legitimation is likely to concentrate more upon whether it should continue to attract educational resources than on detailed discussion of specific content areas, although it may well be that public perceptions of its content will determine the extent to which the subject receives public support.

Physical Education, Sport and Recreation

It is important therefore to identify the way in which physical education is legitimated by providers of resources and other significant publics. Much debate within the profession has centred upon the nature of physical education and upon those features which distinguish it from allied categories such as sport and recreation. To describe a physical education programme as one of recreation, or to suggest that the children are doing little more than playing, is to denigrate it, the implication being that a teacher should have skills which are superior to those possessed by a recreation officer. The Physical Education Association's (PEA) official policy statement is unequivocal about the need to retain the distinction between physical education and physical recreation:

> Physical education within the context of the school, is a structured programme of educational experiences and is not synonymous with recreation.

Sport usually refers to competitive sport and often to high level competition. As such it is seen to be the province of the coach, whose purpose is perceived to be a narrower one than that of the teacher who pursues a multiplicity of objectives. Those working within physical education thus view tendencies to define physical education as synonymous with sport or recreation with some concern. However it could be argued that these are the very elements which legitimate the category of physical education and which ensure the subject's survival in the curriculum. Sport and leisure are important activities for the wider public. As a result, the public's support of physical education may well centre upon their views of the benefits of sport and of recreational activity. Despite criticism from within the profession (Almond, 1983) of an undue emphasis on the talented few at the expense of the great majority of pupils, other groups continue to see the school as nurturing sporting talent. Many teachers are, as Morgan (1982) indicates, still under great pressure to achieve sporting success.

> The unfortunate problem of headteachers, governing bodies and others (including some PE teachers) whose major concern is with winning and collecting trophies has increased stress on the individual teachers and the problem of having to maintain or enhance or even establish the school's reputation in competitive

events all add to the pressure.

The report of the PEA Commission of Enquiry suggests that this problem is by no means confined to secondary schools, when it comments on primary PE,

> There is a tendency for teachers to concentrate on the gifted. Concentrating on the better boys, neglecting the other boys and all the girls.

Physical education can never be independent of sport and recreation if it is the latter two concepts which legitimate it for the majority of the wider public.

Indeed, it is the alleged decline in school sport which has given the physical education curriculum such an unusually high profile in the past two years. It has aroused sufficient concern to make the national press (*The Independent*, 18, 19 and 20 November 1986; *The Times*, 14 October and 26 and 27 November 1986), to interest the BBC in making the notorious *Panorama* programme and to produce debates in the House of Commons.

It is worth noting that MPs, themselves debating the issue, appear to be unable to distinguish between sport and physical education. For example, John Carlisle, speaking in the House of Commons on 8 December 1987, made the following comment:

> Now that the Bill (the Education Bill) is to go into committee, we should try to increase the sport requirement in the curriculum from one to two hours a week.

Public interest in physical activity as a recreational pursuit has two sources, first the revival of interest in health and fitness, and second the use of leisure time activity in contributing to social control. Preparation for leisure, with social control on the hidden agenda, is probably associated more with the programmes offered at secondary level, particularly those involving adult games forms which can be continued outside and post school, than with primary physical education.

> There is a growing awareness that sport in its broadest sense is one of the greatest weapons we have to combat the growing number of social problems which exist today. (Campbell, 1984)

Developing an interest in physical activity for its health and fitness benefits is on the other hand very much relevant to the junior school teacher. It is interesting that health-related fitness, as propounded by teachers, has an obvious parallel in the outside world in the work being undertaken by such bodies as the Health Education Council, and in the general public interest in for example the prevention of heart disease. One can only speculate as to whether this particular curriculum innovation would have been so successful had the wider public not already been persuaded (in terms of change in attitude if not at the level of changing behaviour) of the value of an active lifestyle.

Recent evidence suggests that this should be just as much a concern of the junior school teacher as of the secondary physical education staff.

> Unfortunately the evidence indicates that children are not as active as they appear to be, and that habitual activity is seldom of high enough intensity to promote cardio-vascular health. (Armstrong and Bray, 1986)

It is important therefore that the teacher understands the nature of physical education and its relation to sport and to recreation, so that the subject can fulfil its potential as a medium for education. Many examples could be found of influential individuals or corporate bodies who have overlooked physical education in debates about education. Physical education suffers from omission from discussion rather than from a conscious exclusion or from an actual denial of its value. In fact, middle class parents invest enormous amounts of time, effort and finance in providing physical activity opportunities for their children. There can be no doubt that they value physical activities highly. The investment which independent schools make in sports facilities is also a good indicator of the value attached to involvement in these activities, as is the promotion of individual schools' facilities in their publicity material. It is also interesting that they frequently market their facilities under 'sport' and 'leisure' labels. There may be a lesson here if we wish to 'market' physical education to parents, governors and LEA officers.

Physical education, of course, uses many of the same activities as sport and leisure, but for a different purpose and with differing teaching methods and priorities in terms of outcomes. A couple of examples will suffice to illustrate this point. In contemporary elite sport winning is all. In education this is not the case. If the price of winning is bad behaviour then, in the educational context, that price is too high. Recreational activities, by definition, involve participation from choice. This can clearly not be the case if the teacher wishes all pupils to gain from perceived benefits from a particular activity. Sport and recreation are generally concerned with playing games according to adult rules and conventions. The teacher, particularly the teacher in the junior school, needs the flexibility to adapt and change game structures or to allow children to create their own games so that the experiences provided for the children are appropriate to their age, ability and developmental level.

Teacher Perceptions of Physical Education

At a more practical level, it is interesting to note that in a survey of primary teachers (Williams, 1983) physical education was ranked third in importance behind maths and English, for junior school pupils. Even allowing for sampling bias, this suggests that the subject is accorded rather more than marginal status by many junior school teachers. However, these teachers did value the subject for reasons that would probably not accord with those propounded by physical education specialists and in some cases for reasons which would not be deemed educational.

> I see it in two ways. The first is as a bit of a release from academic work. (male, aged 26–30)

> You can't expect children like ours to sit at a desk and work all day because they're just not capable of it. (male, aged 26–30)

These teachers all value physical education lessons and would not want to see them curtailed or removed, although one would perhaps question the educational content of the work carried out. Others clearly felt that the lessons contributed something to the child's quality of life which would otherwise be missing because of circumstances at home.

> I think children down here wouldn't do much if they didn't have physical education — they sit around and watch TV a lot. (male, aged 20–25)

> Many children in this school come from flats where there are very few facilities for any kind of outdoor life. I think TV keeps a lot of children indoors. (Deputy Head)

A number of the teachers interviewed felt that a structured programme was important both for physical development and for the development of motor control and skills.

> It's important for their physical development — they're growing children. (male, aged 50+)

> I feel that I have to spend a lot of my time in my physical education lessons doing small games, developing their hand-eye coordination. (male specialist)

> I think it's very important — it's part of their physical development isn't it? (female, aged 31–35)

Many teachers mentioned social development as an important benefit to be derived from physical education. Much of this value lay in the fact that children were more mobile than in the classroom, and, thus, situations arose which would not occur during the classroom lessons.

> They're very much areas of social training. To my way of thinking, physical activities are very good for children in this respect. (male, aged 26–30)

> It's a great socializing lesson, to compete well and fairly in a team — it has tremendous social effect. (male, aged 26–30)

> I like to think that when a child learns to play a game with nine or ten other children and play that game well and derive a lot of satisfaction from it, that you're developing a cooperative spirit in that child — you're developing a responsibility to other people. (male, aged 26–30)

> Things show up in games, making the teacher aware of social problems that might not be spotted in other areas where they're sitting in the classroom. (Deputy Head)

Many teachers felt that the opportunity to see children in a different situation, meant that many, who would never achieve high academic standards, had a chance to shine. Several felt that the compensation thus offered was one of the greatest values of physical education.

> It's necessary to make the most of somebody who has a natural ability. You develop that ability, just as you'd develop an ability in maths or English. (female, aged 30–35)

> It gives those who are not very gifted in academic subjects the chance to show some potential in something. (male, aged 26–30)

Children who can't do certain skills in the classroom have a chance to shine in physical education. (female, aged 30–35)

A number thought that physical education was underrated in many schools and that teachers failed to appreciate its value.

I think it's a very much neglected and second rate subject and it shouldn't be, because there's as much to be gained by a child from these subjects as there is from any other. (female specialist)

I still consider it a very important subject. Physical activities have got to go hand in hand with mental activities, and too often this doesn't happen. (male, aged 31–35)

Certainly this sample of teachers would endorse physical education as a universal curriculum subject. It is also clear that, just as perceptions of physical education of many outside education differ from the perceptions of those within education, so the perceptions of the junior school teacher, responsible for the whole curriculum for one class of children, differ from those of the subject specialist. What then do we mean by physical education and what is its relationship with allied activities such as sport and recreation?

Educating the Physical

The paradox with which we are faced is that while it is the physical nature of the subject which gives it its distinct identity and its unique place in the curriculum, it is this very physical nature which places it at the periphery of the curriculum. One consequence of this has been that the contribution of physical education to aspects other than purely physical ones has sometimes been emphasized to the exclusion of its central purpose.

The one essential feature of physical education, that which distinguishes it from all other curriculum subjects, is its focus on the body and on physical experience. It is therefore concerned with the acquisition of movement experience and with education 'of the physical'. The 'physical' nature of the subject should not be underestimated or ignored, for, if we can only justify physical education in terms of its contribution to other areas of experience, then we fail to justify its continued presence in the core curriculum. This may seem to be an obvious point to make but it is one which has sometimes been lost amid a plethora of so-called 'educational' aims and objectives to which physical education is claimed to contribute.

Earlier this century no such difficulty existed: the importance of the physical education programme was stated quite unequivocally to be its effect on the health and physical development of the child. The point has been made elsewhere (Williams, 1987; Kirk, 1988) that improved standards of living, health and diet have altered the meaning of 'health and fitness' as aspirations within physical education, and, that as a consequence, the contemporary focus upon health and fitness cannot be compared directly with that which was found in the 1920s and 1930s.

Furthermore, those children who were educated in independent or grammar schools received a rather different physical education diet. Here the games playing tradition had pride of place, with the emphasis firmly placed upon moral and personal qualities which were thought to be developed through the playing of team games.

Nevertheless, it was the demise of health and fitness considerations in physical education during the early post-war years which changed the focus of physical education significantly. Improved living standards, the birth of the Welfare State and the more equitable distribution of food brought about by wartime and early post-war rationing all played their part in raising health standards among children.

The physical education world saw the opportunity to contribute to more than physical development in the changing educational climate. This new emphasis was articulated in *Moving and Growing* (Ministry of Education, 1952). Anxious to secure the place of physical education on 'educational' rather than 'physical' grounds, aspects such as moral, social, intellectual or cognitive development were subsequently stressed to such an extent that Wright (1977) suggested that the pre-war concern and responsibility for the pupils' welfare had been unduly compromised. Others also commented on the demise of strenuous physical exercise from physical education lessons and questioned the wisdom of this trend (Stevens, 1975; Rowe, 1978; Mawdesley, 1978).

We shall therefore examine first of all how the 'physical' nature of physical education contributes to the educational process. The framework proposed by Arnold (1979) is a useful one for analysis of physical education in terms of its identity as an educational activity. He identifies three dimensions in which physical activity (or movement which is his chosen term) can be an educational medium. These are:

(i)   education IN movement; Physical devel.
(ii) education THROUGH movement; cross - curricular
social, emotional etc.
(iii) education ABOUT movement;
intellectual, physiology etc.

These dimensions can provide us with a range of possibilities in terms of physical education's place in the curriculum. Whether the curriculum attempts to balance all three, or whether one is dominant, will depend on the educational philosophy of the school.

Education 'IN' movement or 'of' the physical takes place through the experience of physical activity. It can only take place through active participation by experiencing the activity concerned. It means knowing how to engage in various physical activities and involves a belief that such activities are in and of themselves worthwhile. If we believe in the value of education in physical activity for the junior school child then we believe that, by giving the child the experience (and the skills necessary for that experience) of movement activities, we are introducing him/her to a 'physical' dimension which should be included in education for its intrinsic value and for the satisfaction which such movement experience can bring. The junior school child wishes to discover what his/her body can do and therefore has a keen interest in physical activity and is easily motivated by challenges of a physical nature. Young children enjoy movement for its own sake and delight in mastering physical skills. To omit the physical dimension from education for this age group, other than for utilitarian purposes, would be to omit a whole category of human experience which is of central significance to many people.

Objectives related to the education 'in' movement dimension could include those concerned with all the physical skills which are prerequisites for participation in organized physical activities, the tactics and strategies which are needed if skills are to be used appropriately, and expressive objectives, which are generally discussed in the context of the aesthetic elements of physical education, although Kirk (1988) points out that they could equally well apply to any activity which is providing opportunity for the development of ingenuity and imagination.

These objectives cannot be pursued without actually taking part in the activities. They will lead to the mastery of a range of physical skills such as body management skills in gymnastics and swimming and ball skills such as throwing, catching, kicking, heading and striking.

Education 'THROUGH' the physical or 'through' movement refers to the use of physical activity as a means of achieving educational ends which are not an intrinsic part of the activity.

Arnold suggests that aesthetic, social and moral development are three aspects of education to which physical activity may contribute. The notion of education 'through the physical' underpinned the public school games playing tradition and was very prominent in the 1950s, when the promotion of physical education as a subject which could contribute to more than physical development was at its height. Indeed the change in curriculum label from PT to PE was a symbol of the subject's contribution to education 'through physical activity' superceding earlier syllabuses which had limited themselves to education 'in or of the physical' through physical training exercises.

For the junior school teacher, education through the physical can provide a valuable cross curricular dimension to the subject. This aspect of physical education is facilitated at primary level by the fact that the teacher is with the class the whole time. Objectives in this dimension may take two forms. First, educational objectives in other subject areas may be achieved through the medium of the physical education lesson. An obvious example of this relates to language development. Physical education provides many opportunities for the repetition and reinforcement needed for language development. Language can also be used in a context, and for a purpose, when working in pairs or groups in collaborative learning situations. Many mathematical concepts can also be either introduced in physical education, or the physical education lesson can reinforce or provide practical examples of concepts introduced in the classroom. There are, for example, many opportunities for measuring or estimating. Health-based work in physical education gives the opportunity to undertake scientific investigative work.

The second way in which physical education can educate 'through' the physical medium is in its contribution to achieving the purposes of education which are not allied to subjects or to areas of knowledge or experience, and which might be described as instrumental or utilitarian rather than educational.

They are nevertheless commonly acknowledged to be important aspects of formal education. Maybe the best and most frequently recognized of these purposes is personal and social development. As already noted, primary teachers identify social development as an important aspect of physical education. Children can learn to share, to work cooperatively and to respect others.

Arnold's third dimension, education 'about' the physical, refers to the study of concepts, rules and procedures involved in physical activities whether these activities be highly structured as in team games, or spontaneous as in the physical play of the young child. It is therefore concerned with understanding and intelligent performance, two concepts which have a high profile in current discussions about curriculum content. Both health related fitness and the understanding approach to games teaching are very much underpinned by beliefs in the importance of education about the physical. This dimension also encompasses the study of physical activity drawing upon areas such as anatomy, physiology, biomechanics, psychology or sociology which is the province of work in upper secondary and higher education rather than in the primary school.

In relation to educating children about movement, many objectives are conceptual, to use Arnold's word, that is, about understanding of what an activity is about. Conceptual objectives can be achieved without participation in that it is quite possible to have a conceptual grasp of 'hockey' or 'rugby' without actually playing the game. It would be however naive to suggest that this conceptual grasp would be anything but limited without some participation. The notion of conceptual objectives which are pursued alongside other participatory objectives is one which is fundamental to contemporary curriculum developments.

It is the conceptual grasp and the understanding which accompanies the activity which is one of the features distinguishing current initiatives in health related fitness with earlier fitness work which simply required children to follow instructions and carry out certain exercises. Similarly, Bunker and Thorpe's philosophy of games teaching demands that alongside practising games skills and playing games, a conceptual grasp of the nature of the game and of game strategies should be developed.

While wanting to stress the artificiality of separating out either dimensions of physical education, or types of objectives, into discrete categories, a clear understanding of their nature can help us in considering the physical education curriculum at the individual level. The contribution of physical education to the education of children with special needs is discussed later in this book. It is worth pointing out here that where children cannot, for whatever reason, take an active part in the lesson, they can be exposed to non-participatory elements of the curriculum and can gain knowledge and understanding.

One further point should be made about the interconnections between these categories. It should be understood that if physical education is to achieve its potential as an educational medium, the curriculum must be planned so that a range of objectives is included. It is not enough simply to expose children to various physical activities and hope that a whole host of outcomes will automatically ensue. In relation to personal and social education through physical education Facey (1984) has pointed out that there have been very few explicit statements about the role of physical education in the personal and social development of young people. He suggests that personal and social education is too important to be left to an intuitive uncoordinated approach which assumes that such things will somehow just happen as part of the hidden curriculum of the school. If areas such as personal and social development are to be more than possible by-products they must be consciously planned for, and experiences structured in such a way that qualities to be promoted are acquired by the child.

The Physical Education Programme

Physical education is often defined in terms of the activities which make up the school programe. In one school, PE is 'football, and gymnastics'; in another it might be 'netball, rounders and dance'. In fact these activities are more properly described as the means by which the ends of physical education are achieved. They will always be specific to a particular school or type of school. Having said this, there is probably much more common ground in terms of activities pursued in the junior school than would be found at secondary level where there is a far greater diversity of facilities and resources available. The DES publication *Movement* does describe the physical education programme for the primary school in terms of the activities which one might expect to see, namely gymnastics, dance, games, athletics, swimming and outdoor activities. These core activities are clearly linked with the areas of experience described by HMI with reference to the 11–16 curriculum, as one would expect given that the junior school is laying down foundations upon which the secondary curriculum will build. These areas are as follows:

(i)   Areas in which the main aim is the development of skilful body management.
           Gymnastics and swimming relate to this area.

(ii)   Areas in which the main aim is creating or being involved in an artistic experience through bodily movement.

This is achieved through dance.

(iii) Areas in which the main aim is competition between groups or individuals involving the use of psycho-motor skills.

This area clearly relates to games playing, although in stressing competition, the use of cooperative games seems to be overlooked, which would be a particularly unfortunate oversight in the context of junior school physical education. The concept of winning and that of one single winner is developed during the primary years and will be of little relevance to the young child.

This area, therefore, would need to be modified to take account of the developmental level of the child but also in the interests of balance between competitive and cooperative activity.

(iv) Areas in which the main aim is body training leading to increased powers of strength, stamina, endurance and a general feeling of well-being.

This is not an area which receives any great emphasis in *Movement*, however the health-based work now being introduced into the junior school is very much related to it. It is perhaps a criticism of much prescription about junior school physical education that this area has been neglected, although it does of course have to be included with due regard for the effects of physical growth and development on the child's physical capacities.

(v) Areas in which the main aim is to meet challenging experiences in varying environments.

This is, of course, experienced through outdoor activities.

The advantage of this description of the activities of physical education is that it is applicable to all schools and to a wide range of circumstances.

Summary

In the school context, physical education is part of the educational process. It must, therefore, both make its own unique contribution to this process, and share and contribute to the achievement of aims across the whole curriculum. It is also closely related to, although not synonymous with, sport and recreation, and, in the junior school context, may be seen as a basis from which interest and involvement in sport and recreation can develop. Public interest in sport and recreation should be seen as beneficial to physical education as a curriculum subject, and should be harnessed to the advantage of work done in schools without prejudicing the nature of the subject as an educational activity.

References

ALMOND, L. (1983) 'Health related fitness', *British Journal of Physical Education*, 14, 4.

ARMSTRONG, N. and BRAY, S. (1986) 'The role of the physical education teacher in coronary prevention', *Trends and Developments in Physical Education: Proceedings of the VIII Commonwealth and International Conference on Sport, Physical Education, Dance, Recreation and Health*, London, Spon.

ARNOLD, P.J. (1979) *Meaning in Movement, Sport and Physical Education*, London, Heinemann.

CAMPBELL, S. (1984) 'The Sports Council and physical education: Partners in development', *British Journal of Physical Education*, 15, 2.

DES (1970) *Movement*, London, HMSO.

DES (1978) *Curriculum 11–16*, London, HMSO.

DES (1987) *The National Curriculum*, London, HMSO.

FACEY, P. (1984) *Physical Education for Life: A Framework for Developing the Physical Education Curriculum*, Coventry, Elm Bank Teachers' Centre.

HARGREAVES, J. (1977) 'Sport and physical education: Autonomy or domination', *Bulletin of Physical Education*, 13, 3.

HENDRY, L.B. (1976) 'Survival in a marginal role. The professional identity of the physical education teacher' in WHITEHEAD, N. and HENDRY, L.B. (Eds) *Teaching Physical Education in England, Description and Analysis*, London, Lepus.

HIRST, P.H. (1974) *Knowledge and the Curriculum*, London, Routledge and Kegan Paul.

HOUSE OF COMMONS (1987a) *Education Reform Bill*, London, HMSO.

HOUSE OF COMMONS (1987b) *Hansard*, 8 December, London, HMSO.

KIRK, D. (1988) *Physical Education and Curriculum Study*, London, Croom Helm.

MAWDESLEY, H. (1978) 'Physical education — An obituary', *Bulletin of Physical Education*, 14.

MEYER, J. (1980) 'Levels of the educational system and schooling effects' in BIDWELL, C.E. and WYNDHAM, D.M. (Eds) *The Analysis of Educational Productivity*, Cambridge, MA, Ballinger.

MINISTRY OF EDUCATION (1952) *Moving and Growing,* London, HMSO.

MORGAN, I. (1982) 'Rugby football in Wales — Some issues and questions', *Bulletin of Physical Education*, 18, 3.

PETERS, R.S. (1966) *Ethics and Education*, London, Allen and Unwin.

PHYSICAL EDUCATION ASSOCIATION (1987) *Physical Education in Schools, Report of a Commission of Enquiry*, London, PEA.

ROWE, H. (1978) 'Whatever happened to physical education?', *British Journal of Physical Education*, 9.

SCHOOL SPORT FORUM (1988) *Sport in Schools*, London, Sports Council.

STEVENS, R. (1975) 'In place of confusion', *British Journal of Physical Education*, 6.

WHITE, J. (1973) *Towards a Compulsory Curriculum*, London, Routledge and Kegan Paul.

WILLIAMS, E.A. (1980) 'Intention versus transaction — The junior school physical education curriculum', *Physical Education Review*, 3, 2.

WILLIAMS, E.A. (1987) 'Health and fitness in the physical education curriculum: Regression or progress', *Health Education Journal*, 46, 3.

WRIGHT, J. (1977) 'Total health: A jubilee perspective', *British Journal of Physical Education*, 8.

Chapter 3:
Physical Education for the Early Years of Schooling

Chris Rose

An examination and review of published literature of early years physical education reveals that very little has been written about human movement and infant practice to guide teachers in schools. It is these teachers, of course, who share the responsibility of establishing firm foundations upon which others build and help our children to grow and flourish as members of our society.

All that we know about human beings living together tells us that there is an unquenchable and compelling need to express ourselves and much of what we regard as central and valuable to our culture and civilization, comes from meeting this need. The most obvious manifestations of this are found in our music, literature, theatre and art. Human movement is just as important. The expressions of movement may be found in games of street and playground, in open and faraway spaces, on the playing fields or on the stage. All are important and are an integral part of each other. John Barnes, Imran Khan and Daley Thompson are no less important to our understanding than Markova, Olga Korbut or Wayne Sleep.

Our children are born free and an important part of that freedom is the birthright of play. Play is an essential part of our children's growth into adulthood. Teachers in schools must exploit and harness that urge to play and provide children with a wide range of movement experiences. There is an enormous responsibility, therefore, to provide children with activities which develop bodily and manipulative skills, an expressive communication of feelings, independent thought and a joy of movement for movement's sake.

Whilst young children make use of movement for many general reasons, they participate in it for its own sake, using it in many ways. When they run they may get somewhere, when they walk it might be along a tree trunk or narrow plank, a jump may carry them over a slab or drain, a climb may take them up a tree, a puddle will offer attractions of feel and sound. An open space will set them off leaping, skipping, shouting, whirling and twirling their arms and participating in all sorts of antics. If there is something on which to climb and swing, anything through which to crawl or creep, then most children will swarm round like bees round a hive. Movement in various guises provides challenge and excitement, but it is essentially intuitive and is an integral part of children's natural growth and development.

Through their natural desire to move, young children will find personal meaning which will contribute to the quality of their lives. They experience the feeling of enjoyment and satisfaction which is aroused by movement, which motivates further participation and they develop emotionally, learning to cope with frustration and tension. They begin to persevere, to persist and develop their powers of concentration, constantly needing success to spur them onward. Through experiences with movement and play, young children mix with others. They observe other children's behaviour and reactions, discover how friendships are made, and gradually become aware of evolving relationships. Play stimulates the child's use of language and the spoken word is often enhanced with gesture and movement.

Young children engage in physical activity which contributes to their physical development. Their sheer appetite for physical activity, the urge to master and exploit the body's capacity for movement, extends their powers of endurance. Children rarely stop, and then only to draw breath, before testing themselves further to delight in physical accomplishments. Through their capacity to learn through movement, children become able to adapt to all sorts of varying situations that are presented to them. They move and respond to control their bodies in the world around them. They learn to adjust to the unexpected, to regulate their body positions in relation to obstacles and to the movement of other people. They learn to dodge, twist, turn and avoid and will propel or project themselves in relation to objects and barriers, to increase their bodily skills. Sometimes they fail, there may be a fall, a bump and tears.

The basis of the physical education programme in the early years is the application of an understanding of the needs of children and their natural patterns of growth and development. It is important for teachers to recognize these needs and plan appropriate material to satisfy them. Movement is intrinsic and its component parts provide the content of the work in physical education. Through involvement with well-planned and balanced work, children will increase in self-awareness, skill and resourcefulness.

A rationale for the development of a physical education programme may look something like Figure 3.1.

Learning Through Movement

Children learn through movement and the process of this learning is the same as any other activity in the infant/first school. They need time to explore, experiment and repeat in order to realize their capabilities.

Exploration underpins and continues throughout the whole of this learning process or mistakes will be made, but recognizing these will often result in more comprehensive learning by the children than if they had been shown a short cut by a well meaning adult. Children enjoy repetition. They will demand 'again, again': the same story, with insistence on the same words. Similarly, they will repeat an action or a routine until it becomes part of themselves. They need the sense of security and success which repetition ultimately provides.

As they develop and become more skilful in movement, children will begin to adapt and refine their skills. They modify movements which have been learned previously in different situations and by refining and adapting them, achieve efficiency and control. Later, they will relish structured situations which are provided to enable them to vary and improvize their actions. They will be able to compose sequences or patterns in a personal way and the teacher will quickly tell by the involvement how appropriate these opportunities are. (See Figure 3.2.)

The Physical Education Programme

The difficult task for teachers is to prepare and teach a series of physical education lessons which respect children's uniqueness and individuality and develop their natural urge to move, so as to improve bodily skills,

Figure 3.1: The place and purpose of physical education for children in their early years

1 Movement is natural for all children.

2 Children have an urge to play and be active.

3 They are curious and want to explore.

4 They find satisfaction in making and creating something which is theirs.

Physical education provides unique opportunities to:

1 Foster these needs.

2 Encourage participation through the joy of movement.

3 Fulfil a child's entitlement to sample a range of experiences which enhance personal qualities.

Through first-hand experiences, provided to fulfil the potential of physical education in four key areas:

1 Expressive movement.

2 Movement extended to large apparatus.

3 Games and small apparatus.

4 Movement in water.

By using themes, tasks and lesson ideas which provide a variety of opportunities for action, challenge and quality.

Enabling pupils to:

1 Learn about 'me'.

2 Achieve understanding.

3 Recognize improvement . . . thereby achieving personal satisfaction.

WHICH DEVELOP

(a) the satisfaction of succeeding;
(b) their ability to communicate and share ideas, express emotions and feelings;
(c) their ability to use curiosity and inventiveness;
(d) their awareness and sensitivity to others;
(e) a sense of belonging and cooperation. Learning tolerance and fairness;
(f) their ability to concentrate and persevere;
(g) opportunities to remember, learn and build on previous experiences;
(h) their ability to lead and be led;
(i) strong bodies that can support themselves;
(j) supple, flexible bodies, that can bend, twist, stretch and turn;
(k) agile bodies that can leap, tumble, swing and balance;
(l) bodies that can sustain periods of physical activity, developing strong hearts and lungs;
(m) coordination and timing so there is poise and control;

        coordination of hand and eye

(n) manipulative dexterity

        bodily skills – adapting to the expected and unexpected.

Figure 3.2: Learning through movement

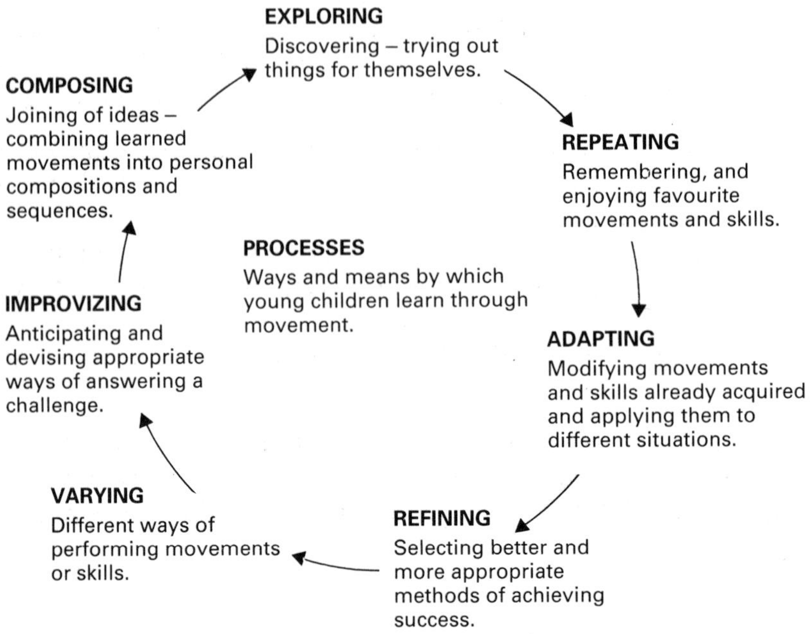

EXPLORING
Discovering – trying out
things for themselves.

COMPOSING
Joining of ideas –
combining learned
movements into personal
compositions and
sequences.

REPEATING
Remembering, and
enjoying favourite
movements and skills.

PROCESSES
Ways and means by which
young children learn through
movement.

IMPROVIZING
Anticipating and
devising appropriate
ways of answering a
challenge.

ADAPTING
Modifying movements
and skills already acquired
and applying them to
different situations.

VARYING
Different ways of
performing movements
or skills.

REFINING
Selecting better and
more appropriate
methods of achieving
success.

help them to think for themselves, grow in stature, agility and strength and contribute to the development of their confidence, self-esteem and regard for others. Whilst an awareness of these considerations is important, so too is a need to understand movement principles. The teaching of movement has been strongly influenced by Rudolf Laban, who lived and taught in England from 1938 to 1958. The basic understanding of his systematic analysis of movement is necessary for all teachers, for it provides the framework for the observation and development and progression of children's work. When Laban began to apply his ideas to the teaching of dance, he organized the way he viewed movement into sixteen basic movement themes. His purpose was to provide teachers with a methodical foundation, on which to build work. It would be unwise to suggest that all his themes were suitable for physical education lesson material with young children and wrong to make assertive statements by saying which were appropriate. This would deny opportunities to some children or be inappropriate for others. Some of Laban's themes lend themselves more naturally to dance movement than they do to games, for example. There is a need for flexibility and adaptability according to the needs and abilities of children and to the requirements of teachers.

In simple terms, it is the opportunities for movement and the logical development of that movement which should determine the course of the lesson. Movement can be developed simply in the following ways:

(a) What you do — actions of running, jumping, skipping, kicking, throwing, stretching, etc. using different body parts and body shapes.
(b) How you move — quickly, smoothly, slowly, lightly, etc.
(c) Where in the space around you? — up, down, forwards, sideways, etc. to the right or left.
(d) With? — in relationship to: a partner, a group, or an object or apparatus.

These are the four aspects of movement and any movement can be defined in these terms by asking: What is the action or the part of the body involved? What is the quality of action? Where does it go in the space?

Lesson Planning

The actions associated with the acquisition of personal and movement skills provide ideal lesson material and action words, and therefore, can provide a framework for the development of lessons. In each lesson, however, there should be four key objectives, which are listed as follows:

1 Activity

Recent alarming evidence that coronary heart disease can become manifest in children from a very early age, makes it essential that children's natural urge to move energetically is satisfied. We need to let children move without too much interruption so that heart rate is increased and activity sustained. Flushed cheeks and beads of perspiration are healthy signs and less teacher talk may be necessary! There are many opportunities to generate activity in physical education, for example, running and chasing games, skipping, travelling quickly without pause, darting, dashing, whirling, twirling, leaping and springing, moving through water quickly and increasing distances.

2 Variety

This is the spice of life it is said, and nonetheless important for young children. This doesn't mean a liberal sprinkling of a variety of activities at the expense of depth, structure and balance. Variety can be developed in many forms and is usually obtained in a number of ways, generally through changes of level, speed, weight, flow, awareness of the spacial dimension, good use of body parts and relationships and sensing when a change of activity is necessary. The teacher's ability to maintain interest in lessons comes largely as a result of being able to provide variety.

3 Quality

It can be truthfully stated that we tend to underestimate children's abilities in almost everything we do and with young children we can demand a great deal. They need to stretch and extend their bodies, especially fingers, toes and necks. Control, poise and tension need to be developed and movement should be dynamic and vigorous. Good body awareness and sensitive use of time, space and weight are sound objectives, but above all, children need to understand the nature of tasks that are set and these should be appropriate to their needs. In games, the smoothness and flow and coordination of bodily actions in relationship to the apparatus being used is something to be prized. In particular, the development of tolerance, fairness and cooperation are desirable objectives.

4 Challenge

All children need to be challenged in the sense that their learning should be differentiated to equate their individual needs. In physical education activities, children need to be extended both physically and mentally and it is important to help children develop the skills of concentration and perseverance. As they grow older, an ability to work alongside and with others in pairs and groups is particularly important.

Diagramatically, satisfying key objectives in lessons will look like this.

Figure 3.3: Lesson planning: Key objectives

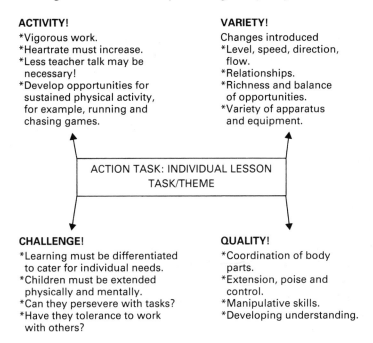

ACTIVITY!
*Vigorous work.
*Heartrate must increase.
*Less teacher talk may be
 necessary!
*Develop opportunities for
 sustained physical activity,
 for example, running and
 chasing games.

VARIETY!
Changes introduced
*Level, speed, direction,
 flow.
*Relationships.
*Richness and balance
 of opportunities.
*Variety of apparatus
 and equipment.

ACTION TASK: INDIVIDUAL LESSON
TASK/THEME

CHALLENGE!
*Learning must be differentiated
 to cater for individual needs.
*Children must be extended
 physically and mentally.
*Can they persevere with tasks?
*Have they tolerance to work
 with others?

QUALITY!
*Coordination of body
 parts.
*Extension, poise and
 control.
*Manipulative skills.
*Developing understanding.

When planning lessons, it is helpful to provide a framework in which to develop themes and ideas and it is suggested that each lesson should be planned around eight key questions which are designed to take the lessons from a series of stages to a logical conclusion. However, every lesson which is taught may vary considerably depending upon the reactions and responses of the children in the class. Suitable questions are listed as follows:

★ *What Am I Trying To Do?*

This question focuses on the purpose of the lesson and its objectives. Some of these will relate to developing areas of knowledge, particular skills and to personal qualities.

★ *Tasks I Might Set?*

The tasks are designed to fulfil the objectives and purpose of the lessons.

★ *How Might I Begin?*

This question focusses on suggested starting points. It is always a good idea for the teacher to set the task in the classroom so that work can begin immediately upon entry into the movement area. Since much of the work in the early years is exploratory, a good deal depends upon children's initial responses to ways in which they commence the lesson. Drawing upon and developing children's starting points is not easy, but is nevertheless very important.

★ *Look! What are the Children Doing?*

When planning lessons it is interesting to reflect on how children might respond to the initial task. Whilst it is difficult to forecast outcomes, some idea of what the children are likely to do or not do is an important element of planning.

★ *How Can I Help?*

On the basis of using forecasted outcomes, it is then helpful to provide means through which guidance may be offered to improve individual, group and class responses.

★ *Developing the Lesson*

Teaching points can be provided in this section to pursue ideas further, extend the tasks and stimulate progress.

★ *How Did it Go? Questions to Ask*

On the basis of the planned lesson and children's response, it is helpful to pose a series of questions which enquire about task setting and achievement of the original objectives so that an evaluation of the teaching/learning experiences just offered the class can be undertaken.

    ★ *Where Do I Go From Here?*

It is always necessary to be able to plan further work so that development and progression can be ensured.

Areas of Movement Experience

Physical education provides unique opportunities to fulfil a child's entitlement to sample a range of experiences which enhance personal qualities. Through first-hand experiences which are provided to fulfil the potential of physical education, four key areas are suggested. These are expressive movement, that is movement which evokes a dance-like response, movement extended to large aparatus, that is movement which is more objective in which the body is inverted and allows natural activities to be extended to the use of large apparatus. The third area is that associated with the development of games skills and the playing of games whilst the fourth key area is the development of movement skills in water.

Expressive Movement   DANCE.

The essence of expressive movement lies in an instinctive desire to use movement as a means of self-expression and communication. Using movement in this unique way, children can say, this is me — this is what I am! Young children need to move expressively and teachers have exciting opportunities to help their charges awaken their senses and to tune their bodies. They should help the children discover the entire range of bodily movements and develop ways in which sensitivity and awareness can be fostered. With careful teaching, children will begin to appreciate different qualities in their movement and the various ways of using space. Later, some children will respond to others and the teacher may wish to extend this new-found ability to work with a partner or group. The language of movement is important and stimulating children to move in response to a sensitive choice of words will require careful consideration. Other forms of stimuli present themselves, but these must be chosen wisely and at appropriate stages during the children's development. Careful teaching will generate a growth of sensory perception, which will help the children develop an understanding of themselves and others.

Use of stimuli

There are several stimuli which can be used to promote and develop quality in expressive movement, but the one already familiar to the children, namely the teacher's voice, is the most effective. Careful thought needs to be given to the choice of words that will stimulate the desired quality in children's movement, for example, 'spiky, sharp, jerky or smooth, calm, flowing'. However, as with all our language and conversations meaning is not only conveyed by what we say, but how we say it. The voice is an extremely versatile instrument.

The use of percussion or extracts of well-chosen music may add spice, excitement, variety and interest to the work. If percussion instruments are to be a really effective source of stimulus for movement, then the children need to be given many opportunities to perfect their skill in using these instruments before they are able to appreciate the range of sounds. The teacher should also experiment with these different sounds and should only consider using good quality instruments which give a clear and precise response. Working with percussion should begin with a teacher using the instrument in conjunction with a group of children and impact is gained when the teacher and the instrument form a definite part of the movement. It should be used when the teacher feels it will enhance language, for example, 'sudden, sustained, strong, etc.,' or in order to add interest and refinement.

Short passages of well-chosen music can add interest, excitement and quality to movement. Choice is essentially personal and considerable time may be taken in making a final selection. Generally speaking, music should be chosen for three distinct purposes. Firstly, it may be used for travelling or to help the children to use space effectively. A lively, rhythmical piece of music may be appropriate to encourage a variety of steps, jumps and turns for example. Secondly, parts of a piece of music can be selected to help the children develop particular movement qualities, for example, the feeling of sustained, strong, sudden or light. Finally, music can create a mood or an atmosphere providing an appropriate setting for an extended piece of movement work.

Lesson ideas

As previously mentioned, teachers can develop expressive movement lessons around the careful choice of action words. A number of these are listed below:

ACTION TASKS FOR EXPRESSIVE MOVEMENT

The whole body moving — travelling on feet
Run and pause
Stride and freeze
Skip and settle
Dash, dart and fade
Understanding body parts
Bending and stretching
Turning
Twisting
Twisting and turning
Stretch and turn
Swing — stretch and turn
Leap — land and freeze
Balance and over balance
Jerky and smooth
Strong and light
Sudden and sustained
Straight and curved
Up and down
Leaping and falling
Rolling and stretching
Working with my partner — meet and part
                               — lead and follow
                               — join and separate
Working with my group

Figure 3.4: Lesson examples – satisfying key objectives in expressive movement

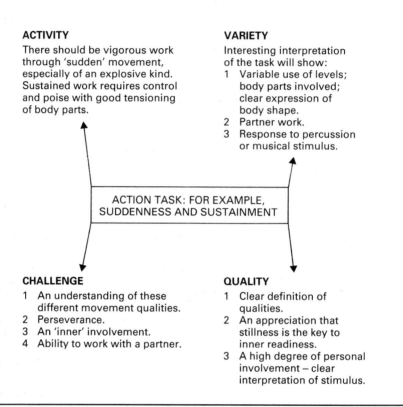

ACTIVITY

There should be vigorous work through 'sudden' movement, especially of an explosive kind. Sustained work requires control and poise with good tensioning of body parts.

VARIETY

Interesting interpretation of the task will show:
1 Variable use of levels; body parts involved; clear expression of body shape.
2 Partner work.
3 Response to percussion or musical stimulus.

ACTION TASK: FOR EXAMPLE, SUDDENNESS AND SUSTAINMENT

CHALLENGE

1 An understanding of these different movement qualities.
2 Perseverance.
3 An 'inner' involvement.
4 Ability to work with a partner.

QUALITY

1 Clear definition of qualities.
2 An appreciation that stillness is the key to inner readiness.
3 A high degree of personal involvement – clear interpretation of stimulus.

Action Task: 'Suddeness and Sustainment'

Teaching Considerations
No matter how skilful and supple children are, without attention being paid to effort qualities, expressive movement is likely to be expressionless. 'Sustainment' is a difficult quality to obtain in young children who are naturally energetic and lively. The highlighting of suddenness makes expressive movement very exciting and it is a real challenge for teachers to be able to obtain success in contrasting these two qualities.

What Am I Trying To Do?
* To help the children master not only the ability to move suddenly and with sustainment, but to adjust mentally and physically in changing between these effort qualities.

What Tasks Can I Set?
* Sustained movement can be developed through activities such as opening, bending, stretching, turning. A cymbal softly played can help to develop this feeling of smoothness and slowness.

* Real suddenness is a particularly difficult quality to achieve and imagery may be necessary, for example, a flash of lightning, switching on the light. Movements with individual parts of the body may help develop suddenness, for example, opening and closing the hand, a sudden flick of the fingers.

How Might I Begin?
Ask the children to move slowly and sometimes quickly and to concentrate on the difference in speed. Allow time for experimentation.

Look! What Are The Children Doing?
In many cases, there will be very little difference in the changes. It will be important to look at and discuss some of the quick movement. If any child shows suddenness, this could be a starting point.

Develop suddenness by asking the children to change shapes. The children can attempt to arrive at a new shape suddenly.

What Help Can I Give?
The stillness which completes the sudden change of shape should become an inner preparation for the next sudden action.

The teacher's voice and choice of words should help the children to experience this inner feeling of readiness.

If children are expected to persevere with suddenness for too long, any quality they have gained will degenerate into hasty movement which lacks control. This development can be provided by compensatory movement, for example, 'show me a favourite way of moving slowly and then make a surprise, sudden movement'.

Developing the Lesson
The children will need some compensatory movement and disussion will help to talk about smooth, controlled slow movement.

Emphasize watching a small part, for example, hand moving smoothly. This can be extended to encouraging the whole body to move slowly and smoothly, for example, turn or a roll. This work requires concentration.

Allow the children the self-discipline of selecting from and using both qualities. If creativity is lapsing due to their concentration on the quality, a spatial idea may spark the children off again, for example, travelling with sustainment and staying in personal space for sudden movement.

If the children are ready, they will enjoy responding to a percussive stimuli, for example, a tambour sharply beaten, contrasted with the skin being scratched very slowly.

N.B. It is important that the children develop the qualities of suddenness and sustainment before percussion or a musical stimulus is used.

How Did It Go?
Often children show a distinct preference for one of these qualities. Usually, it is one which they perform most easily and express their personality. It may be that concentration was lacking for this work and as such, much work will need to be repeated.

Chris Rose

It will be important to develop these qualities. Alert, highly strung children need to feel sustainment. Placid children need to become alert.

This may be a good stage for children to begin using percussion themselves. They may lead groups of sudden movers or sustained movers. (This must be short or the quality will degenerate).

Older children may enjoy partner work, responding to each other's change of quality. Group shapes can be built by children entering suddenly or with sustainment.

Areas Extended to Large Apparatus Work

Young children love to run, climb, jump and roll. They are attracted by obstacles upon which they can hang and swing, scramble over and leap off. As they grow older they will try a variety of activities and accomplish numerous individual feats of skill which are personally satisfying. Movement extended to large apparatus provides opportunities to develop these experiences, through the varying challenges presented by apparatus of different textures, widths and heights. The young child's urge to move and explore can be satisfied in this way.

Large apparatus should always be seen as an extension of children's movement experience and not as a separate 'climbing' lesson. The greatest safety element one can develop in children is consideration for and awareness of others. It is important to provide sufficient time so that these tasks can be completed in a thoroughly satisfying way.

Children should be taught how to handle apparatus, lift and carry it correctly and safely. Portable equipment must be carried, never dragged and children should look where they are going. The youngest infants may need help from their teacher to move the heaviest and highest apparatus, but from early stages they should be taught how to carry and set up the equipment. Children should be encouraged to lift pieces into position after preliminary floor work and apparatus provides a natural extension of work begun on the floor. Lessons should contain a satisfactory balance of floor work and work on apparatus. The two are complementary. It is useful to remember:

APPARATUS FOR THE LESSON, NOT A LESSON FOR APPARATUS!

Action tasks for movement extended to large apparatus

As with expressive movement, a number of action words can provide most appropriate lesson materials and these are listed below.

Travelling on feet
Travelling on hands and feet
Travel and pause
Rocking and rolling
Shapes — long, wide and curled
Stretching and arching
Curling — stretching and arching
Building bridges
Taking and holding weight
Jumping and landing '
Jumping and landing — variety of shapes in the air and different take offs
    and landings
Jump — land and turn
Balance and turn
Balance and roll
Up and down
Symmetry and asymmetry
Travelling with variety
Quick and slow
Directions and pathways
Sequences — short and simple
Working with my partner — meet and part
                                  — over/under and around

Sample Lesson Plan: Movement Leading to Large Apparatus

Action Task: 'Travelling on Hands and Feet'
Teaching Considerations:
The ability to take body weight on the hands is very important, for very few, if any, young children are able to take all their weight on their hands for any length of time. They are well able to distribute their weight on a variety of combinations of hands and feet.

What Am I Trying To Do?*
Encourage the children to become confident in taking weight on hands and feet.
* Develop skilfulness in using these parts of the body.
* Develop strength in upper body parts.

What Tasks Can I Set?
* Travel about the hall on hands and feet — back facing the floor — stomach facing the
  floor.

* Travel on two hands one foot — one hand two feet — one hand one foot.
* Place hands on the floor and jump feet into the air.
* (More confident children can try to balance on their hands.)

How Might I Begin?
Travel about the hall on hands and feet in different ways, but try not to crawl!

Look What Are The Children Doing?
* Some children will lack confidence to take weight on hands at all.
* Look for and praise interesting movements that show variety.
* Provide individual help to those trying to take weight on hands — 'Strong hands and arms'.
* Encourage bunny hops to begin with then from a position with hands on the floor kick one leg upwards until a more confident action is achieved.
* Develop the work on the floor by setting further tasks mentioned above.

Developing the Lesson on Apparatus
* Use hands and feet to get on and off the apparatus.
* Use hands and feet to travel, along, over, across and off apparatus.
* As 2 above and then travel in interesting ways to another piece of apparatus.
* Balance in stillness on hands and feet with good stretching shapes and controlled actions.

What Help Can I Give?
* Try to work with individuals praising and encouraging both confident children and those more timid pupils.
* Show examples of interesting work.
* Encourage good use of the floor as a link between pieces of apparatus.
* Insist on quiet work, plenty of activity and no queues — the floor is the best and biggest piece of apparatus!

How Did It Go?
* Was the task too easy/difficult for the majority of children?
* Was there variety? Was the work all at one level — in one direction?
* Did I sufficiently challenge the most able?
* Did the tasks inhibit the flow of movement?

Where Do I Go From Here?
* Repeat a part or parts of this lesson as necessary — this work will require consolidation over a period of time with young children.
* Encourage greater variety: movement on/off apparatus
                           movement over/along/under
                           balance and stillness
                           variety of speed, direction and level.

Figure 3.5: Lesson examples — satisfying key objectives. Movement leading to large apparatus (gymnastics)

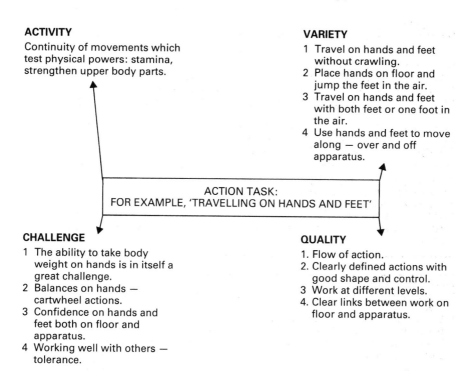

ACTIVITY
Continuity of movements which test physical powers: stamina, strengthen upper body parts.

VARIETY
1 Travel on hands and feet without crawling.
2 Place hands on floor and jump the feet in the air.
3 Travel on hands and feet with both feet or one foot in the air.
4 Use hands and feet to move along — over and off apparatus.

ACTION TASK:
FOR EXAMPLE, 'TRAVELLING ON HANDS AND FEET'

CHALLENGE
1 The ability to take body weight on hands is in itself a great challenge.
2 Balances on hands — cartwheel actions.
3 Confidence on hands and feet both on floor and apparatus.
4 Working well with others — tolerance.

QUALITY
1. Flow of action.
2. Clearly defined actions with good shape and control.
3 Work at different levels.
4. Clear links between work on floor and apparatus.

Games and Small Apparatus

No-one can doubt the appeal of games to children, for they are a natural extension of play. They provide opportunities for children to pit their wits, test their physical powers and extend their relationships. In the young child we see the very essence of games playing, the excitement of chase, the expectancy of capture, the miming and acting out of situations, the triumph of mastery over man-made objects. Children play and make up games to satisfy the needs of the moment. Their actions are spontaneous and all-absorbing. It is this spirit and fun of playing which should be the dominant feature of games and small apparatus for children in their early years, for the chief ingredient in any game is the element of play, utterly fascinating because it is so incalcuable.

Figure 3.6: Action tasks for games and small apparatus

Early Stages		
Free play (Choose and play)	Free choice (Choose one piece and play in many ways)	Restricted choice (Choice is limited)

↓

Running and chasing games

↓

Activities Requiring Help

(Work from the above will show the teacher where help is required)

Skipping — Catching — Stopping — Hitting — Throwing — Aiming — Kicking — Heading

↓

Later Stages

Skilfulness in the above activities will enable confident children to play games with others either in twos or threes.

Making and inventing games — target games

Fielding and stopping games — games over a 'net'

Running and passing games

Unlike any other area of the movement programme, games provide opportunities to develop special manipulative skills and dexterity, for the body has to adjust itself continually to all the variable uncertainties of moving objects. Chances for developing individual qualities also manifest themselves in games with the essential ingredients of play, challenges, vigorous physical activity, cooperating with others and learning to be tolerant and fair. The sensitive and caring teacher who knows and understands children will be able to interpret the fundamental appeal of games and be able to use them to develop personal qualities in children.

The game programme

In the very early stages, children will need considerable opportunities to play alone. They will require time to gain confidence in their play and to

Figure 3.7: Lesson examples: satisfying key objectives. Games and small apparatus

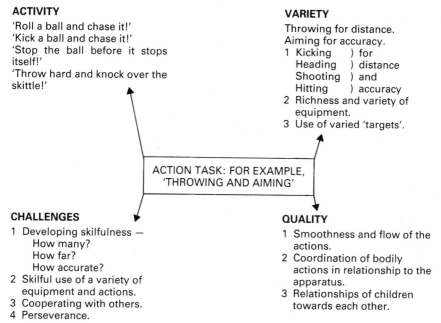

ACTIVITY

'Roll a ball and chase it!'
'Kick a ball and chase it!'
'Stop the ball before it stops itself!'
'Throw hard and knock over the skittle!'

VARIETY

Throwing for distance.
Aiming for accuracy.
1 Kicking   ) for
  Heading   ) distance
  Shooting   ) and
  Hitting   ) accuracy
2 Richness and variety of equipment.
3 Use of varied 'targets'.

ACTION TASK: FOR EXAMPLE, 'THROWING AND AIMING'

CHALLENGES

1 Developing skilfulness —
  How many?
  How far?
  How accurate?
2 Skilful use of a variety of equipment and actions.
3 Cooperating with others.
4 Perseverance.

QUALITY

1 Smoothness and flow of the actions.
2 Coordination of bodily actions in relationship to the apparatus.
3 Relationships of children towards each other.

experiment with equipment and apparatus before any instruction is given. This time is important for the children and gives a teacher opportunities to observe and assess their progress. From free play activities, children will wish to practise a number of activities which interest and excite them. It will soon become evident which these are and the teacher must be ready to help them progress. It is important to help children create games out of these activities rather than allow them to practise skills in a repetitive fashion. The fun involved in playing games must be paramount. As the children grow and become more skilful and competent, they will begin to combine these skills. They will start to play alongside their friends more and more working cooperatively to achieve success. They will enjoy playing games in small groups of twos and threes and should be encouraged to make up their own games in which they use their new found knowledge and skills. Much later, this type of play could become more competitive, for children may wish to compete one against the other. This is an important part of the games programme and must be encouraged. Children's natural desire to run and move must not be neglected and they should be encouraged to play some of the traditional games which are their heritage.

Sample Lesson Plan: Games and Small Apparatus

Action Task: 'Throwing and Aiming'
Teaching Considerations
Target games will enable children to develop the skills of aiming, hitting and throwing. In the early stages, aiming will be concerned with the careful placing of an object in an attempt to achieve accuracy. In early throwing activities the emphasis should be placed upon obtaining a good rhythmical action, rather than trying to develop accuracy which is a very advanced skill for very young children.

What Am I Trying To Do?
Provide the children with opportunities to apply the skills of throwing, hitting and aiming in a number of games and activities.

Develop the coordination, timing and manipulative skills associated with these activities.

Provide a number of chances for children to enjoy success, thereby helping to develop confidence and self-esteem.

What Tasks Can I Set?
Activities in which individual children can throw or aim at targets.

How Might I Begin?
Encourage children to work in spaces away from each other, playing an aiming or throwing game, for example, 'choose a hoop to throw bean bags into', 'choose a skittle at which to throw bean bags'. How many can you score?

Then, 'now gradually try to move further away and see if you can still hit the target'.

Look! What are the Children Doing?
Aiming and throwing may be awry, especially if some time has elapsed since these activities were tried.

A variety of successes will be evident — some children will need to stay close to the target; others will be able to quickly reposition further away quite quickly.

Some children may be throwing towards one another, and in their excitement may not have been aware of safety factors. (All throwing activities require plenty of space and throws should be in the same direction). If a class activity is conducted in throwing, children should retrieve the object at the same time. Objects to be thrown should be carefully chosen, for example, bean bags, air flow and foam balls which are less likely to injure).

What Help Can I Give?
Work with individual children to reinforce teaching techniques associated with throwing and aiming.

Provide help to the less able and challenge the better pupils. 'I am sure you can go further away from the target'.

Aiming may require special help. It is important to give the object, 'plenty of air', by tossing it upwards rather than directly at the target.

Developing the Lesson
Change over from throwing to aiming. Some children may need more time to develop these skills, others can be given further challenges;

1 *Individual Activities*
* Throwing or hitting a ball at a target on a wall. The rings of the target can have different values.

* Goals can be kicked or hit at with bats and hockey sticks. The goals can be narrowed to make the task more difficult.

2 *Partner Activities*
* Rolling a ball between skittles or cones.

How Did it Go?
How well did the children respond to the variety of tasks? Could they cope with the numerous skills which were required? Were they challenged sufficiently? Did they persevere with the task? Was enough time given to the less able to consolidate the basic skills?

Where Do I Go from Here?
Repeat parts of much of this lesson as necessary. Time is important if skills are to develop.

A number of small group games for example, 'Defend the skittle' and 'Keep the basket full'. Encourage individuals and partners to experiment in developing in their own target games.

Movement in Water

For many children, water has magical qualities and an irresistable fascination. They love the sensation of warm water in the bath at home — they play with a variety of toys, blow bubbles, splash and experiment with a range of movement activities. Young children stamp their feet with joy in puddles and play for hours with water whether it be in a gutter, a tube, a tub, a bottle or a container. These kinds of experiences are both pleasurable and important and provide a valuable forerunner to swimming.

The majority of children will love to feel that they can swim easily and efficiently. To achieve this degree of efficiency however, will take some children a considerable time and in the early years at school there may well be very limited opportunities for children to obtain access to a swimming pool. Wherever possible, children should be encouraged to visit a swimming pool and it helps considerably if the mother or father can enter the water with them. For some children, however, this may never happen and where schools have pools of their own or access to pools, a visit to the site to observe their older friends in action is a valuable learning experience. Children learn much by watching others and being encouraged by their peers to experiment and practise.

'Every child a swimmer', is an ideal naturally well worth adopting, but what do we mean? In the early years, it is felt that children should be allowed to enjoy being in water where it is hoped to instill in them certain qualities, skills, habits and knowledge. They should gradually learn about flotation, buoyancy, moving, submerging, breathing easily and in a controlled manner. They should be able to control their movements, coping with expected and unexpected situations. They should feel safe and secure in a water environment. Above all, we must try to ensure that they are eager and excited to enter the swimming pool whenever possible. With children in their early years, the teacher will need to focus upon individual progress and practise. Developing enjoyment and confidence, and eventually swimming, will depend upon the ability to maintain a relaxed posture in the water using the natural buoyancy and rhythmical action of limbs in movement.

Developing lesson ideas

In common with all other areas of the curriculum, children will be at different stages of learning and have individual needs. Lesson ideas can be grouped as follows:

1 Early beginnings

All children need to explore a new environment in their own time. Whether they are familiar with a swimming pool or not, some children will take quite a time to get used to the new situation, the scope of the pool, the depth and temperature of the water. Early lessons should be designed to help children to become familiar with and develop confidence in this new environment.

2 Play with a purpose

A series of lessons could be planned to help the children develop further confidence and freedom of movement, thereby overcoming the novelty of moving in a strange medium which presents problems of preserving and recovering balance. It is important to structure games to suit the needs and particular anxieties of the pupils. For example, timid children should not be asked to participate in games where they will be subjected to splashing, being bumped or likely to fall over.

3 Moving through the water

In this group of lessons, emphasis should be placed upon helping children to discover how readily water supports them and how the movement of different parts of the body in different ways helps them to achieve flotation and propulsion. The purpose is to build confidence so that they can achieve control in many situations in a relaxed and unhurried manner. The foundations of swimming will be based on a carefully structured beginning.

ACTION TASKS FOR MOVEMENT IN WATER

Early Stages
1 Visit the pool.
2 Get in the water!
3 Getting wet!

Play with a Purpose
1 Blow and go.
2 Water games.
3 Wading and stepping.

Moving through the Water
1 Floating.
2 Push and glide.
3 Sculling.
4 Multi-stroke movement.

Sample Lesson Plan: Movement in Water

Action Task: Push and Guide
Teaching Considerations
By now, the children should be familiar with the water, know that their bodies can keep them afloat, be more confident and able to adjust to expected and unexpected situations.

They will want to participate in activities which bear close resemblance to 'real swimming'. Eventually, the aim will be to teach them recognized strokes and so it is necessary to help them place their bodies into more 'streamlined' positions.

What Am I Trying To Do?
Help the children to become confident and skilful in gliding in a horizontal body position on both front and back with their heads 'immersed' in the water. To prepare them for more advanced skills by helping them to understand the importance of developing a good horizontal body position.

What Tasks Can I Set?
* Revise floating skills on both front and back.

* Pushing and gliding activities.

How Might I Begin?
Front or back floating positions — children crouching in the water — chins on the surface. They take a good breath, tip themselves forwards or push gently backwards — pausing for a moment — stretch out arms and legs, lifting their feet into float positions.

* Once the children can assume a good horizontal body position on front and back, they can try the front glide position into the side. They could crouch down, shoulders under the water, chins on the surface of the water, arms in front of them. A good breath is taken and the body tipped gently forwards, with the face placed on the water. One leg is lifted and the body is pushed gently forwards into a glide position.

Look! What Are The Children Doing?
Some may tip or roll over onto their sides. Bodies may stay tucked from the waist, others will be completely horizontal. In the back float, there may be a reluctance to place the head back so the ears are under the water.

Some children will easily manage this activity if they undertake it gently. Others may come up violently out of the water, tense and spluttering!

What Help Can I Give?
Ask the children to spread out their arms and legs gently to stop them tipping over.

Encourage them to lift their feet so they can adopt the straight body position which is important.

The more confident can be asked to repeat the practice trying to increase the distance. Those that are still too tense could repeat the flotation skills as gently as possible before repeating the push and glide. More timid children can try flotation skills with aids.

Developing the Lesson
From the edge of the pool the children can try pushing off the side from the side of the pool first, with one and then two feet. They should adapt an 'arrow shape' which is streamlined, keeping as much of the body in the water as possible. Aim for distance.

As above, but encourage them to breath out gently as they go forwards.
Back Glide
Repeat the procedure for front glide. They should tip gently backwards with their arms at their sides. The head must not be thrust too far back or they will go under. Ask them to look 3for a spot at the top of the pool side.

How Did it Go?
Have the children confidently mastered the glide on both front and back (the back glide is much the harder)? Can their bodies achieve a streamlined effect?

Are they able to breathe out as they glide on their tummies?

Where Do I Go From Here?
Back glides can be attempted from the pool side — arms holding the rail, feet tucked up on the wall — head back.

Glides can be attempted rolling from front to back and then to front and so on? 'How many rolls can you do as you glide across the pool?'

Push and glide activities front to back and then to front and so on? 'How many rolls can you do as you glide across the pool?'

Push glide activities can be practised to music which has sustained qualities, for example, Vangellis Opera Sauvage 'Hymne', Polydor, 3574 — 140. Sequences can be made in which front and back glides can be linked together with turns and rolls.

Figure 3.8: Lesson examples: Satisfying key objectives in movement in water

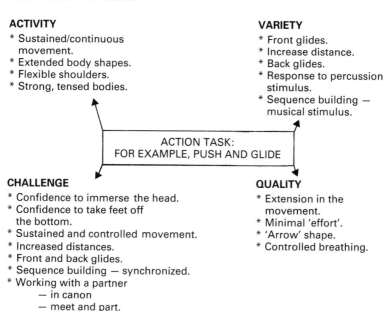

ACTIVITY
* Sustained/continuous movement.
* Extended body shapes.
* Flexible shoulders.
* Strong, tensed bodies.

VARIETY
* Front glides.
* Increase distance.
* Back glides.
* Response to percussion stimulus.
* Sequence building — musical stimulus.

ACTION TASK:
FOR EXAMPLE, PUSH AND GLIDE

CHALLENGE
* Confidence to immerse the head.
* Confidence to take feet off the bottom.
* Sustained and controlled movement.
* Increased distances.
* Front and back glides.
* Sequence building — synchronized.
* Working with a partner
    — in canon
    — meet and part.

QUALITY
* Extension in the movement.
* Minimal 'effort'.
* 'Arrow' shape.
* Controlled breathing.

Conclusion

Our children have an entitlement to rich experiences which satisfy their thirst for knowledge, their acquisition of skills and provide opportunities to grow and develop as responsible people. Physical education through the medium of movement experiences offers enormous scope for the personal development of young children. Their movement is an integral part of themselves, they require opportunities to utilize, develop and enjoy it. Let them move!!!

Chapter 4:
Health-related Fitness for the Primary School

Stuart Biddle and Grant Biddle

Introduction and Rationale

One of the major developments in British physical education in the past decade has been the growth in health-related fitness (HRF). Although work along these lines has been consistently in evidence in the USA since the 1950s, British physical educators have, until recently, been relatively slow in reacting to the health needs of the nation. Where HRF courses have been developed, they have usually been taught with students in the later years of compulsory secondary education. Although wider 'health' concepts are often taught with younger pupils, there is little evidence of systematic teaching of HRF in primary schools or of suitable provision in pre- and in-service primary teacher education.

The purpose of this chapter, therefore, is to define HRF, provide a rationale for its inclusion in primary education, and to suggest a variety of practical methods for teaching HRF across the primary curriculum.

What Is Health-related Fitness?

The term physical fitness is used a great deal, yet it is often poorly defined and understood. Figure 4.1 shows the different component parts of physical fitness.

Caspersen, *et al* (1985) define physical fitness as 'a set of attributes that people have or achieve that relates to the ability to perform physical activity' (p. 129). The phrase 'have or achieve' suggests that some

Figure 4.1: Component parts of physical fitness

```
        ┌──────── PHYSICAL FITNESS ────────┐
        ▼                                   ▼
HEALTH-RELATED                      PERFORMANCE-RELATED
cardiorespiratory fitness           agility
strength                            balance
muscular endurance                  coordination
flexibility                         speed
body composition                    power
stress management                   reaction time
```

aspects of fitness have to be acquired whereas others are 'given'. In terms of achieving the health benefits of physical fitness, one has to *achieve* improvements in cardiorespiratory fitness, muscular strength and endurance, flexibility, and body composition, as shown in figure 4.1. These components are health-related because if improvements are made in any one of these aspects of fitness, it is possible to enhance health and prevent disease. For example, cardiorespiratory exercise is important for weight control and aerobic conditioning. These are both important in the prevention of coronary heart disease (CHD). Similarly, low back pain and poor posture can be related to weak muscle strength and poor flexibility, and high levels of body fat are usually associated with general inactivity. The skill- or performance-related aspects of fitness, however, are more related to athletic performance, and although can be improved with training in some cases, are not generally associated with health benefits. As Caspersen *et al* say the 'health-related components of physical fitness are more important to public health than are components related to athletic ability' (*ibid*, p. 128).

The Relationship Between Physical Activity and Health

If we wish to educate children in matters of health, an emphasis must be placed on health-related fitness components. There are several advantages of doing this. First, aspects of HRF can be improved by all children regardless of physical ability. Indeed, the greatest changes will be seen in those children who need the greatest help (for example, the obese). The health benefits from physical activity are achieved by *doing* physical activity, not necessarily by achieving a high level of athletic excellence or physical fitness relative to the next person. Many other factors (some of which are hereditary) will affect physical fitness *performance* (for example, time taken for a distance run). In short, it is the *process* of activity that has health benefits, not the *product* of being athletically gifted or better than someone else. For example, Seb Coe would be quite likely after months of inactivity to still be able to defeat a keen, but relatively untalented, jogger over 800 metres. While Seb Coe may have excellent qualities of speed and endurance (due in part, most likely, to hereditary factors), and thus be able to run fast even without training, the *health* benefits will accrue to the jogger, not to an inactive Coe.

Second, current lifestyles are such that one of the most urgent health problems facing our society is that of inactivity. Such health problems are called 'hypokinetic' as they are caused by, or related to, a lack of physical activity. Hypokinetic problems can include CHD, obesity, hypertension (high blood pressure), hypercholesterolemia (high blood cholesterol), osteoporosis, diabetes, back pain, postural defects, stress, anxiety and depression. The influence of physical activity on some of these conditions will vary between conditions and individuals. Many of these conditions, because they are related to lifestyle, are the product of habit and socialization. We are strongly influenced by the behaviours of our parents thus suggesting that education for health should start from the first day of life, not the fifth year in secondary school. Certainly it is too important not to be taught in primary schools (see Bray, 1987; Pangrazi, 1987).

In addition to the rationale based on physiological health, there is growing evidence for the beneficial effects of exercise on mental health. Dishman (1986) lists the available evidence on exercise and mental health:

1 physical fitness is positively associated with mental health and well-being;
2 exercise is associated with the reduction of stress emotions such as state anxiety;
3 . . . exercise has been associated with a decreased level of mild to moderate depression and anxiety;
4 long-term exercise is usually associated with reductions in traits such as neuroticism and anxiety;
5 appropriate exercise results in reductions in various stress indices such as neuromuscular tension, resting heart rate, and some stress

hormones;

6 current clinical opinion holds that exercise has beneficial emotional effects across all ages and in both genders (pp. 331 – 2).

There is also preliminary evidence that changes in self-esteem for children are more positive after fitness activities compared with other physical pursuits (Gruber, 1986). It is also common for adults to report 'feeling better' after exercise, although little research concerning this has been done on children.

Are Children Active Enough?

If physical activity, based on the health-related components identified in figure 4.1, is so important for health, are children adopting the right lifestyles by being active enough? This is an educational and public health issue that has received relatively little attention in Britain, although exploratory work by Dickenson (1986) suggests that children in the English West Midlands are generally quite inactive. A more formalized approach has been adopted in the USA where studies have been conducted to test the physical fitness of American youth. However, as suggested earlier, it is more important to consider indices of health-related *activity* rather than just levels of fitness performance. Recent American studies show that for children of both primary and secondary school age body fatness has increased significantly over the past two decades (Brandt and McGinnis, 1985; Ross, *et al*, 1987). Whether this is due to a decline in physical activity, an increase in caloric consumption, or both, remains to be determined. However, in society generally, we tend to have a slightly *reduced* caloric consumption than a few years ago, yet levels of body fatness have increased. This would suggest that activity levels have actually declined.

Figure 4.2 shows data from Gilliam, *et al* (1981). In this study, the researchers continuously monitored forty children, aged 6–7 years, for a twelve-hour period. The graphs in figure 4.2 clearly show the relative inactivity (as measured by heart rate) of these children, and in particular the girls. It is often recognized that cardiorespiratory fitness benefits will accrue when heart rate is elevated. Only twenty minutes of the time for boys was spent at a heart rate above 161 beats (75 per cent of maximum), and less than ten minutes was spent at this level for girls. This is unlikely to induce great changes in cardiorespiratory fitness for girls. However, one should not make the mistake of equating HRF only with elevated levels of heart rate. Other significant health benefits, such as fat control, can be achieved with more moderate, but prolonged, activity levels.

Promoting Health and Fitness

The need for significant changes in the public health is well known. However, the role of physical activity is often, in the opinion of the authors, not stressed enough. A major review of the link between CHD and physical inactivity recently stated that the evidence was such that a *causal* link could be proposed (Powell, *et al*, 1987). In the United States Department of Health and Human Services (1980) 1990 health objectives for the nation, eleven are concerned with physical fitness and exercise (Powell, *et al*, 1986), including a call for a greater number of children being involved in *daily* physical education. The success of such a programme, without loss of academic performance, has been demonstrated in Australia (Dwyer, *et al*, 1983). In Britain, there has been an increased recognition of the role of exercise, but even in the latest public health policy documents (for example, King's Fund Institute, 1987), the mechanisms for implementing such changes are poorly discussed. The 'Heartbeat Wales' programme, on the other hand, clearly spells out the need for health-related fitness in schools and the population at large (Heartbeat Wales, 1987). Now is certainly the time for all educators to make their contribution to individual well-being. HRF has a sound research base, greater than any other aspect of physical education, and as such the case for educating young children for health and fitness is a compelling one. Attitudinal factors also dictate that a great deal of health education is too late if left to the secondary school. The primary years are potentially where the greatest impact can be made.

HRF in an Interdisciplinary Context

Many educational reports and surveys over the past fifty years have emphasized the importance of physical education in the overall development of the child and, more recently, the DES National Curriculum Consultation document (DES, 1987) has recognized that physical education should be one of the 'foundation subjects', although the time

Figure 4.2: Heart rates of 6–7-year-olds

BOYS

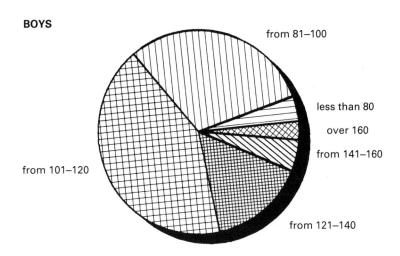

GIRLS

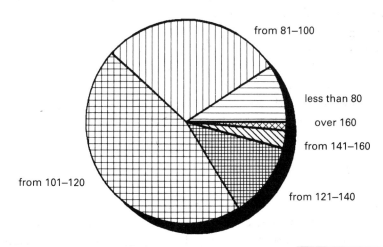

Source: Gilliam, *et al*, 1981.

allocation remains a problematic issue of debate. Given this philosophical commitment to physical education in policy documents, PE in primary schools must be seen as an integral part of the curriculum and not as a 'break' from classroom work. It is not an isolated subject and its relevance to the *total* curriculum should be continually emphasized since there are many natural links that can be made with other areas.

It is important that all children receive a 'balanced' PE programme. This will, of course, be dependent on such factors as facilities, expertise and equipment, although some balance between games, body management (for example, athletics, gymnastics, swimming), creative activities, outdoor education, and health-related fitness should be achievable in all schools.

Practical Teaching Ideas

The above comments suggest that physical education in the primary school cannot take place in isolation from other areas of the curriculum. Indeed, HRF is ideally placed to contribute to worthwhile and enjoyable cross-curricular projects for all children. In the document *Health Education from 5–16: Curriculum Matters* (DES, 1986), a statement headed 'health education across the curriculum' referred to the role of physical education:

> In physical education important health matters arise in a variety of ways, not least through its focus on body management and control . . . Many PE teachers stress the importance of looking after one's own body and the need for suppleness, stamina and strength, and in recent years there has been a growth in work explicitly concerned with keeping fit. This work can . . . include discussion about fitness, discovering how muscles work, the possible relationship between exercise, health and physical fitness, and encouragement to pupils to continue some form of physical activity when they leave school. (p. 13)

In this section of the chapter each area of HRF is explained alongside practical examples of activities. Suggestions are then made as to possible links with other areas. For reasons of space, only examples can be given. However, it is hoped that teachers will find enough information to develop HRF activities in their own teaching environments. Those interested in further reading in each aspect of HRF are referred to Biddle

(1987), Biddle, Mowbray and Benfield (1989) and Corbin and Lindsey (1985).

Stamina

The word stamina is used as an easily understood alternative for cardiorespiratory or cardiovascular exercise. It refers to whole body exercise that taxes the heart, lungs and circulation, hence involves large exercises like jogging, cycling and swimming. Improvement in stamina occurs through prolonged aerobic exercise of moderate intensity, such as brisk walking and jogging. This is easily recognized by elevations in heart rate and breathing rate. However, to achieve the health benefits of stamina exercise, it should be prolonged (over fifteen minutes) and therefore cannot be over–intense. Potential stamina exercises include: brisk walking, circuit training, cycling, dancing, hill walking, jogging/running, rope skipping, sports (those of a continuous nature), and swimming.

In teaching stamina exercises in HRF, it is important to tackle the wider issues of *why* stamina is important to health, how the heart (and other body parts) works, how to assess stamina, how to improve stamina, and other tasks. In other words, HRF allows for children to be *educated* in health/fitness. This seems highly preferable to merely 'getting kids fit' through some disciplined process of exercise. It is more important to win the 'war' of lifetime health than the 'battle' of short-term fitness! Table 4.1 gives some examples of how stamina exercises in HRF can link with other curriculum areas.

Figure 4.3 shows a simplified jogging route that can act as both a jogging trail and a diagram of the heart. A more detailed explanation, with developments, can be found in Kern (1987). The idea is that the pupils run along the route and learn the signposts along the way. These signs refer to key parts of the heart and circulation system and can be modified to suit the age group. Children can learn to take their own heart (pulse) rate, record it, graph group scores, discuss why it changes etc. Such activities could easily be incorporated into other PE lessons, such as athletics and games.

Table 4.1: Links between example stamina exercises in HRF and other areas of the curriculum

Physical Education (HRF)	Science and Maths	Language and Humanities	Creative Arts
1 'Blood flow' jogging route (see figure 4.3). Children jog route noting key 'signposts' about the heart, blood and muscles. Vary difficulty according to age. 2 'Stamina name game'. Each child gives her/his name followed by a stamina exercise (for example, jog on spot for eight steps). Each exercise must be different. Class learns full sequence of one exercise followed by the others. 3 Stamina exercise to music. Variations could include children planning exercise to fit the music or bringing their own music appropriate for stamina exercises.	Concepts of human biology – blood, heart etc. Work with models of the heart. Study of lungs and respiratory system. Ageing and stamina. External factors and stamina – smoking, pollution, etc. Science of dehydration and perspiration. Diet and stamina. Illness and exercise. Invent personal stamina test. Class test. Record and plot results. Averages. Age/sex differences. Improvement graphs over time. Pulse rates before and after exercise. Different methods of recording data.	Writing about various jobs that require different amounts of stamina. Writing on sports/pastimes that require different amounts of stamina. Imaginative writing: on the atmosphere at the London Marathon, or mental attitude/thoughts of an athlete prior to a long race. Newspaper report on a marathon. History of the marathon and other endurance events (for example, Tour de France). Route mapping. Stamina vocabulary – for example, fit, far, long. Historical events and stamina – battles, marches, etc. Modern lifestyle and stamina – machines and working practices across the ages.	Models of athletes. Collage of pictures of races. Coloured clothing in a marathon. Clothing design for long-distance events, for example, cycling, running. Design a logo for a local race or club. Dance/drama related to events requiring stamina, for example, expeditions, battles, old workhouses. Music for stamina ('aerobics'); rhythm, classical ballet and stamina. 'Great egg race', devise machine that can work for long periods.

Figure 4.3: Blood flow jogging route

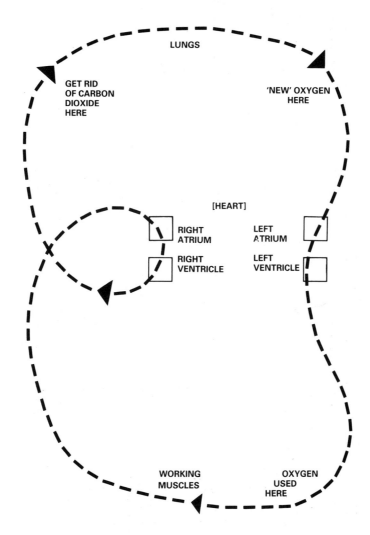

Source: Adapted from Kern, 1987.

Strength

Strength is a simplified term for muscular strength and endurance exercise. From a health point of view it is important to develop and maintain muscle fitness for reasons of back care, posture and specific 'disease' such as osteoporosis in adults. For children, the attraction of good posture and muscle tone (for both sexes) is quite evident, even in young children, and this can be a factor influencing feelings of well-being and self-esteem.

Strength exercises are those where a resistance only allows the exercise to be repeated a few times (about six or less). Since this creates stress at the joints it is generally an unsuitable form of exercise for young children, and certainly the usual forms of strength exercise such as weight training are not to be encouraged in the primary school. Lower intensity exercise, with less resistance and hence more repetitions (muscular endurance) is a suitable form of exercise for this age group. However, care should be taken that the number of repetitions is not excessive or the loading too high (see Dauer and Pangrazi, 1986, for examples of a variety of muscle fitness exercises for young children).

Table 4.2 gives examples of developing muscle fitness exercises in HRF and linking them with other areas of the curriculum. For example, a set of simple endurance exercises could be performed, with or without partner assistance/resistance, and the pupils have to identify the areas of the body (ie muscles) that are being developed. The links between this and, say, the drawing of a body and identifying the appropriate body parts, should be clear. Again, simple muscle endurance exercises can be interspersed in other activity classes, such as during a gymnastics lesson. At all times, the teacher should be emphasizing the correct technique of exercising rather than demanding more effort in an autocratic style that is sometimes associated with the military 'boot camp' approach. Such 'no pain, no gain' methods are inappropriate for the development of positive attitudes towards health and exercise.

Suppleness

Suppleness is sometimes referred to as 'flexibility' and is the amount of movement available at a joint. In practice we refer to flexibility in terms of the ability to stretch the muscles. Although good flexibility is usually associated with specific groups of people, such as dancers, gymnasts and

Table 4.2: Links between example strength exercises in HRF and other areas of the curriculum

Physical Education (HRF)	Science and Maths	Language and Humanities	Creative Arts
1 Partner circuit. In pairs, each perform exercises with either partner assistance or resistance. Include many body parts – for example, push-ups, sit-ups, step-ups, toe-raises, arm circles. Children to identify working body parts. 2 Rhythmic muscle exercises to music. Split into 3 routines: (a) arms + shoulders (b) middle (c) legs.	Model of muscles. Function of muscles. Fulcrums, levers, joints, etc. Strength measures. Pulleys. Weight training equipment. Weights and measures. Safety in lifting. The strength in the animal world.	Vocabulary of strength – heavy, lift, load, weight, pull, push etc. Word games. Order and process of competitions (for example, Olympic weightlifting). Writing on personal experiences involving strength. Jobs requiring strength (for example, circus acts). Drugs in sport – morality. Muscles and men/women – cultural biases. Handicap and muscles.	Sculptures of muscles/bodies. Drawing of muscles. Labelling. Cartoons. Design a poster for 'Worlds' strongest man' contest. Design equipment to help handicapped people. Models of skeleton. Models of machines v. models of humans.

65

swimmers, all people need at least a reasonable degree of muscle flexibility to avoid low back pain and postural problems. Those lacking flexibility are also at greater risk of injury during physical exertion.

Although young children generally have satisfactory flexibility, it is important to teach the benefits and enjoyment of this form of exercise so that it becomes a more accepted part of physical activity in adolescence and adulthood. One only has to observe many recreational exercisers (for example, joggers, squash players, weight trainers etc) to see that flexibility is usually given only brief attention in their routines. Flexibility should be developed and taught in two ways:

i)   as part of an exercise 'warm-up': this should be after some gentle rhythmic exercises which warm the body;

ii) as a form of exercise in its own right.

Improvements in flexibility will come from regular stretching (for example, daily) whereby the muscle is slowly stretched to a point of 'mild tension' then held in that position for up to thirty seconds. This is best done when warm, such as after exercise. Do not encourage bouncing or 'ballistic' stretches as these can be counter-productive or even dangerous. Table 4.3 shows how flexibility exercising might link with other areas of the curriculum.

Given that flexibility exercises should be relatively static, young children may find it difficult to maintain interest in prolonged stretching. It is recommended, therefore, that stretching exercises are performed for short periods of time, but frequently, such as at the beginning of lessons for about five minutes. The use of appropriate music may also help. For a wide range of possible exercises, see Anderson (1980).

Nutrition and the Body

Figure 4.1 shows that 'body composition' is a component part of HRF. Body composition usually refers to the make-up of the body in terms of fat, muscle and other tissues (for example, bone, organs, etc). From a health point of view it is important that children learn about the ways of body fatness control, the mythology associated with certain practices, particularly 'popular' dieting methods, and the role of exercise in weight control. Clearly such topics could be tackled in an advanced form, such as the biochemistry of nutrition. However, appropriate content can also

Table 4.3: Links between example suppleness exercises in HRF and other areas of the curriculum

Physical Education (HRF)	Science and Maths	Language and Humanities	Creative Arts
1 'See for yourself'. Perform flexibility 'test' (for example, sit with soles of feet against wall — legs together and straight). Stretch to wall — how far can you get? Perform five minutes of leg stretching exercises. Now how far can you get?	Pliability of materials. Tests of suppleness of different parts of the body. Different ways of recording results. Disease and suppleness, for example, arthritis.	Vocabulary of suppleness, for example, bend, pliable, elastic etc. Poetry using adverbs to begin each line. Using the project vocabulary to teach adverts, nouns, verbs and adjectives.	Make an instrument for measuring suppleness. Dance routines and suppleness. Drawings depicting aspects of suppleness.
2 Flexibility tests on (a) sit and reach (as above) (b) touch hands behind back- one up, one down. (c) shoulder lift from lying Is there such a thing as 'all over' suppleness? Devise improvement exercises	Machines that measure suppleness; invent your own. Animals and suppleness.	Sports and pastimes requiring suppleness. Jobs requiring suppleness.	
3 Stretch to music. Which type of music is best? Why?			

be developed for primary children. Table 4.4 shows the links with other curriculum areas.

In essence, body fatness will increase when the body receives more 'energy' (food and drink) than it uses (activity). To maintain current levels of body fat, therefore, the energy equation must be balanced. The best way of doing this is through sensible exercise and nutrition habits, not by drastic reductions in food for short periods of time. 'Sensible exercise and eating' should be a central topic for HRF in the primary school, even though only part of it falls into the domain of active physical education. The role of physical activity in weight control can be taught during lessons of an active nature.

Continual assessment of body size (height, weight, girth etc) is likely to be of great interest to young children and a rich source of information for many topics. However, it is clearly an area of potential difficulty since it is dealing with such a personal issue. For example, the measurement of body fatness or girth is likely to be embarrassing to certain pupils. Great sensitivity must be displayed and, where possible, screened areas for privacy should be made available (further issues associated with HRF testing will be discussed later). It should also be recognized that in addition to overfatness, there is a danger of having too little fat. This is particularly hazardous in adolescents who have eating disorders such as anorexia.

Relaxation and Stress Management

An important part of HRF, although not exclusively related to exercise, is the ability to relax and manage stress. It is simply not true that tension and stress is something only associated with adolescence or adulthood. People of all ages can be affected and appropriate stress management and relaxation exercises are important lifetime skills to be introduced at an early age. Although in-service training is badly needed in this area, teachers can begin to introduce the concepts of stress, tension and relaxation (Biddle, 1988). Pupils can discuss various situations that they have faced and how they felt at the time, including prior, during and after different exercises. A simple competitive/non-competitive differentiation is likely to clearly illustrate the different feelings of tension and relaxation in physical activities (see table 4.5 for some suggestions on linking stress management concepts across the curriculum and see

Table 4.4: Links between 'nutrition' and the body in HRF and other areas of the curriculum

Physical Education (HRF)	Science and Maths	Language and Humanities	Creative Arts
1 Perform different types of exercises (for example, run ten mins, walk fifteen mins etc). With help from the teacher, charts etc, how much energy is/was used? Find equivalent energy value food item.	Study of different foods and energy. Human digestive system. Growing food. Import/export of food and drink. Graphs of daily diet (diet log); most/least liked food.	Reporting of diet log and description of foodstuffs. Diet changes in history. Diets around the world. Collection of food labels — place on map. Starvation and the Third World.	Food label collages. Food type collages. Food printing (for example, potatoe, carrott). Dance drama linked to humanities (for example, factory food processes) — use of percussion.
2 Measure height and weight. Is there a relationship (in the group?). Why?	Boys/girls/ages and diet. Animals and diet — herbivores, carnivores. Food labels, ingredients, additives.	Study of farms and farming. Diet and religions. Language of food adverts. Shops and supermarkets. Restaurant menus — healthy?	Drama relating to farming methods. Songs about food and drink.
3 Measure skinfold thickness. Keep records for future *personal* comparison.	History and development of food and medicines. Diet and health.		

Madders (1987) for some excellent ideas of practical exercises for children).

Substance Abuse

Although the area of substance abuse (for example, tobacco, alcohol and drug abuse) is not directly linked with HRF in the PE context, it is nevertheless an important topic to be handled in the curriculum. No details will be given here but teachers are recommended to include this in their teaching of health concepts.

Further Issues

Before concluding this chapter there are some key issues in the teaching of HRF that need further discussion and clarification. The issues to be addressed will be: fitness testing, and involving parents and other teachers in HRF.

Fitness Testing

As interest in HRF has increased over the past few years, so has the use of fitness testing. This is not restricted to schools as health clubs and community health education displays often use fitness tests in their promotions. It is not the intention to discuss this topic in detail but merely to highlight some of the key issues in effectively using fitness tests in a primary school HRF context. For further discussion on HRF testing in schools, see Fox and Biddle (1986 and 1987).

Central to the use of fitness testing with children is the clear identification of the *objectives* of testing. It is the considered opinion of the authors that HRF testing is primarily about *educating* children for health-related fitness. In other words, tests should be used for helping children learn about themselves and HRF. If they satisfy this objective then their use should continue. However, they should not be used for selecting children for sports teams, for public personal comparison (including published lists on notice boards), nor should they be used for grading purposes (although this does not usually occur in the British system even though pressure for such practices is increasing with the

Table 4.5: Links between stress management in HRF and other areas of the curriculum

Physical Education (HRF)	Science and Maths	Language and Humanities	Creative Arts
1 'Play hard-play soft': in pairs, one keeps as hard/tense as possible as the other tries to turn him/her over lying on the ground. Repeat with partner now keeping as soft/loose as possible. Differences? 2 Learn a muscle relaxation exercise. 3 How do you feel after exercise? Run for ten mins (slow). Comment on feelings of tension/relaxation.	Sleep — length, patterns etc. Graphs, averages, times. Taking temperature, 'normal' temperature. Relationship between °C and °F. Graphs showing frequency and types of hobbies, pastimes done for 'relaxation'. Bodily reactions to stress. Computer graphics of the stress response.	Describing personal feelings at times of stress. Describing the stress response. Creative writing — fear, phobias, dreams. Anger and aggression. TV and aggression. Methods of relaxation — hobbies, TV etc. Yoga, meditation etc. Holidays and travel as relaxation. Changes over time in hobbies and holidays. Board games around the world. Advertising alcohol and tobacco.	Restful/soothing music. Drawings of pastimes, hobbies. Dance/drama of aggression, sadness, other emotions. Design of leisure centres. Design of leisure clothes.

adoption of more numerous 'profiling' techniques).

One of the major difficulties with HRF tests, such as a distance run or number of sit-ups, is that the final score is the result of a number of different factors. These factors include motivation, test conditions, maturation level and heredity. This is why comparisons between pupils can be a meaningless exercise if the objective is to educate for health/ fitness. Testing can be usefully employed if pupils can learn something from the tests and monitor themselves over time to see changes in their physical selves. It will be recalled from the earlier section on physical activity and health that it is the *process* of activity that has health benefits and not necessarily the *product* of achieving a high score on a fitness test. In short, fitness tests should only be used as far as they provide an educational tool for children to learn about HRF. If used properly they can provide a rich source of information for the child as well as provide a great deal of material for other projects in such areas as maths and science.

Involving Other Teachers and Parents

In stating our objectives in HRF as the teaching of health/fitness skills *for a lifetime*, we have obviously set ourselves a difficult task. This task will be even harder unless the support of other key people is harnessed. In particular, the success of the school HRF programme is dependent on the extent to which teachers can enlist the support of colleagues, and the effectiveness of HRF on individual pupils is dependent on the level of parental support. For these two reasons it is strongly recommended that the following options be considered:

(i) hold special 'teach-ins' with colleagues outlining HRF, the content of lessons, future directions, pupil responses etc;

(ii) involve colleagues by giving them responsibility for some of the cross-curricula links. For example, if one member of staff is less than happy in the practical environment of the gymnasium or hall, try and get them involved in another area of the curriculum which links with this practical work, as shown in tables 4.1–4.5;

(iii) organize a 'health day' where all school activities are based on the theme of health;

(iv) organize a parents evening on health/fitness showing the work of the pupils and possibly including a mini-lecture and/or slide presentation;

(v) have a health/fitness display unit (for example, tape-slide, video, books, handouts etc) at a parents evening.

Conclusion

In this chapter an attempt has been made to outline the importance of teaching young children about physical activity and health. The tremendous growth in interest in HRF in British PE in recent years seems to have been restricted to the middle and later years of secondary education. This is a mistake as HRF should be taught from the start of schooling. However, in order to assist children to see the 'holistic' nature of fitness and health, a cross-curricular approach is essential in the primary school.

Acknowledgements

Appreciation is extended to Mrs N. Biddle for advising on the 'practical ideas' section of this chapter.

Further Information

Further details of HRF work with primary school children can be obtained from the 'Happy Heart Project', The Curriculum Centre for Physical Education, University of Hull, 173 Cottingham Road, Hull HU5 2EH.

References

ANDERSON, B. (1980) *Stretching*, London, Pelham.

BIDDLE, S.J.H. (Ed) (1987) *Foundations of Health-related Fitness in Physical Education*, London, Ling Publishing House.

BIDDLE, S.J.H. (1988) 'The other 'S' factor: Stress recognition and management', *Bulletin of Physical Education*, 24, 1, pp. 26–31.

BIDDLE, S.J.H., MOWBRAY, L. and BENFIELD, J. (1988) *The Teaching of Health-related*

Exercise: A Manual for Schools, London, Health Education Authority.

BRANDT, E.N. and McGINNIS, J.M. (1985) 'National children and youth fitness study: Its contribution to our national objectives', *Public Health Reports*, 100, pp 1–3.

BRAY, S. (1987) 'Health and fitness in the primary school', *Perspectives*, 31, pp 6–18.

CASPERSEN, C.J. *et al.* (1985) 'Physical activity, exercise, and physical fitness: Definitions and distinctions for health-related research', *Public Health Reports*, 100, pp 126–31.

CORBIN, C.B. and LINDSEY, R. (1985) *Concepts of Physical Fitness* (5th edn), Dubuque, IO, Wm C. Brown.

DAUER, V.P. and PANGRAZI, R.P. (1986) *Dynamic Physical Education for Elementary School Children* (8th edn) Minneapolis, MN, Burgess.

DES (1986) *Health Education from 5–16: Curriculum Matters*, 6, HMI Series, London, HMSO.

DES (1987) *National Curriculum 5–16: A Consultative Document*, London, HMSO.

DICKENSON, B. (1986) 'The physical activity patterns of young people and the implications for PE', *Bulletin of Physical Education*, 22, pp 36–9.

DISHMAN, R.K. (1986) 'Mental health' in SEEFELDT V. (Ed) *Physical Activity and Well-being*. Reston, VA, AAHPERD.

DWYER, T. *et al.* (1983) 'An investigation of the effects of daily physical activity on the health of primary school students in South Australia', *International Journal of Epidemiology*, 12, pp 308–13.

FOX, K.R. and BIDDLE, S.J.H. (1986) 'Health-related fitness testing in schools: I – Introduction and problems of interpretation', *Bulletin of Physical Education*, 22, 3, pp 54–64.

FOX, K.R. and BIDDLE, S.J.H. (1987) 'Health-related fitness testing in schools: II — Philosophical and psychological implications', *Bulletin of Physical Education*, 23, 1, pp 28–39.

GILLIAM, T.B. *et al.* (1981) 'Physical activity patterns determined by heart rate monitoring in 6–7-year-old children', *Medicine and Science in Sports and Exercise*, 13, pp 65–7.

GRUBER, J.J. (1986) 'Physical activity and self-esteem development in children: A meta-analysis' in STULL, G.A. and ECKERT, H.M. (Eds) *Effects of Physical Activity on Children*, American Academy of Physical Education Papers No 19. Champaign, IL, Human Kinetics/AAPE.

HEARTBEAT WALES (1987) *Exercise for Health: Health-related Fitness in Wales*, Heartbeat Report No. 23. Cardiff, Heartbeat Wales.

KERN, K.A. (1987) 'Teaching circulation in elementary PE classes: A circulatory system model', *Journal of Physical Education, Recreation and Dance*, January, pp 62–3.

KING'S FUND INSTITUTE (1987) *Healthy Public Policy: A Role for the HEA*. London, King's Fund Institute.

MADDERS, J. (1987) *Relax and Be Happy: Techniques for 5–18-year-olds*, London, Unwin.

PANGRAZI, R.P. (1987) 'Health-related fitness for young children' in BIDDLE S.J.H. (Ed) *Foundations of Health-related Fitness in Physical Education*, London, Ling Publishing House.

POWELL, K.E. *et al.* (1986) 'The status of the 1990 objectives for physical fitness and exercise', *Public Health Reports*, 101, pp 15–21.

POWELL, K.E. *et al.* (1987) 'Physical activity and the incidence of coronary heart disease', *Annual Review of Public Health*, 8, pp 253–87.

ROSS, J.G. *et al.* (1987) 'The National Children and Youth Fitness Study II: Changes in body composition of children', *Journal of Physical Education, Recreation and Dance*, November–December, pp 74–7.

UNITED STATES DEPARTMENT OF HEALTH AND HUMAN SERVICES (1980) *Promoting Health/Preventing Disease: Objectives for the Nation*, Washington, DC, US Government Printing Office.

Additional Useful Resources

FRASER, K. and TATCHELL, J. (1986) *You and Your Fitness and Health*, Usborne.

My Body — a Health Education Council Project (1985) London, Heinemann Educational Books.

Chapter 5:
Teaching Games for Understanding

Alan Asquith

Introduction

It is a commonplace that the characteristic virtue of Englishmen is their power of sustained practical activity, and their characteristic vice a reluctance to test the quality of that activity by reference to principles. They are incurious as to theory, take fundamentals for granted, and are more interested in the state of the roads than in their place on the map.

To paraphrase Tawney's (1961) (now inappropriately sexist) argument, it does not matter how good one is at building roads, it is more important that they are going to the right places. In this chapter an attempt is being made to see if the general direction towards the journey's end can be improved so that the majority of children reach a worthwhile destination. In other words, in our games teaching are we, the teachers, making the best use of our resources to help all children achieve their optimum potential in the playing and understanding of games? Can we, by changing the focal point of such lessons, from skills and techniques to games making and tactics, improve the environment in which learning might well take place?

Colin Richards (1985) defined the curriculum as 'the medium through which education is conducted in schools. It comprises those educational experiences or courses of study provided by teachers' (p. 1).

This definition in my mind sums up what teachers should be concerned with when planning their games lessons. However, I have found little evidence in either the primary or secondary sectors (Asquith, 1987) that any real attention is being paid to educational concepts in the planning of games lessons, therefore little or no thought is being given to the curriculum. All too often the games lesson starts with an introductory activity, euphemistically called the 'warm up', followed by a skill practice and ending in a game. Yet these same teachers especially in the primary sector, would not follow a similar framework in other areas of the curriculum.

Mauldon and Redfern (1981) pointed out very clearly that the teaching of games in the primary school was out of line with the characteristics and philosophies of teaching in other areas of the curriculum. Rather than foster a child's curiosity and interest through exploration, experimentation and discovery, which in effect is allowing the child to find out for him/herself and solve his/her own problems, the tendency in games teaching appears to be to instruct the child on exactly what is to be done.

Teaching Games Through Understanding

In contrast, if a games-making or understanding through games approach was used then many characteristics and philosophies used in other areas of the curriculum could be brought into use. In this situation the children could well be made responsible for choosing their own sides, electing their own leaders in addition to devising a game within the parameters laid down by the teacher. For example, the children would be responsible for seeing that each game had:-

(i)   a set of rules;
(ii) a method of starting and restarting;
(iii) a method of scoring.

Of course, teacher intervention and/or direction would be inevitable, but equally teachers should be aware that many forms of intervention may well inhibit some of the decision making, problem solving and socializing aspects of the game-making process. At this stage the children are coming to terms with, and through the interactions possibly being socialized into, certain modes of behaviour. By their verbal and non-verbal communication in the games-making interaction the children will settle disputes, deal with 'rule-breakers' and be constantly confronted with 'problematic' situations. In short they are securing a personal and social education *through* the physical as well as education *of* the physical. Below I present two examples from my own research programme to illustrate the point.

Example 1: Approximately five to fifteen minutes into the lesson

This was a group of eight children, seven boys and one girl, aged between 9 and 11 years, involved in a games-making lesson. 'Gloria' constantly held the ball whilst directing operations, changed the rules whenever it suited her and in general appeared to be dominating the game. Gloria was not the most skilled performer in her group, neither was she physically the largest, nor the eldest, she was however very 'bossy'. After much initial argument and dissent by team mates and opposition alike, Gloria had to change her behavioural patterns in order that any semblance of a game could proceed. This was done by group 'pressure', the opposition in particular, by the withdrawal of support and 'goodwill' from the interaction. Little was said after the earlier skirmishes, the majority just did not bother to play properly. Two started kicking leaves at each other, one just stood and gazed into space, two talked a while and then started a chase-type game, leaving Gloria to try to 'organize' the remaining two. There was a great temptation to intervene but as the scenario unfolded it became evident that the change of 'tactics' by peer group members elicited a changed response from Gloria. The interaction, (lesson), was too short for any real evidence to be produced to ascertain whether Gloria's changed behaviour was in fact a new role or a tactical change to ensure her continued dominance of the group. However, a game was devised with group members having a reasonable say in its construction.

Example 2: Approximately twenty to thirty minutes into the lesson

This was a group of eight children, four boys and four girls divided into two teams, each team consisting of two boys and two girls. An entirely different type of problem was highlighted, but I feel there was real evidence of a solution.

Team A were constantly fouling a semi-fixed net alongside their allotted playground area. They felt that they were disadvantaged and complained loudly to team B. So by mutual agreement the two teams changed 'ends' so that now team B were disadvantaged. Still problems, so after further discussion the pitch was 'turned through 90°'. The problem was not yet solved, for the net was still interfering with play. Finally permission was sought and granted for the net to be removed. Problem solved. This episode took approximately eight minutes and much discussion, but the children finally solved the problem themselves.

Fact or Fiction?

Recent research by Bennett (1984) has indicated quite a gap between theory and practice in primary education. The picture is one of conscientious and dedicated teachers failing to match task demands to children's attainments and need levels. Although Bennett concentrated on the 'academic' curriculum, one can easily translate his findings into a typical games teaching situation. How many teachers make any real assessment of the children's games playing ability and teach according to the individual needs of the children? How often is the 'bland and uniform diet' of football, netball and rounders the mainstay of the school games programme? Do we go even further and actually 'teach out' the enjoyable aspects of the game, the fun element which it is believed is inherent in children's games, in other words the reasons for playing? Are the ways we approach the teaching of games stylized adult interpretations of how children *should* play games, how in fact we *would* like them to play games.

The next stage of development might well be for teachers to 'stand back' and allow the children to learn through an understanding approach. For example, allow the children to learn that discussion is not about who can shout the loudest or who owns the ball, but about putting forward a viewpoint, listening to other viewpoints and then reaching a consensus decision. The process is noisy and can take a large percentage of time in the early stages, but is this not part of the educative process in physical education?

Games–Making

Much of the early research work in the field of games teaching has been undertaken by Thorpe and Bunker (1986), Almond (1983), and Spackman (1983) but most of this was directed towards secondary school children. It was Almond's (1983) work on games-making which particularly interested me as it showed possibilities for the primary age range.

In the games-making process the children would create something that was theirs. They would be involved in their own learning, share ideas and work cooperatively, and hopefully find out such things as why rules are important and what purpose they serve. To a certain degree they would be responsible for their own curriculum. The teacher would provide the framework, for example, the type of game to be played, the apparatus to be used, the playing area and so forth, but actual content would, to a large extent, be in the hands of the children.

In the creating of the games, opportunities must be presented for systematic experimentation and problem solving. Within a curriculum so based there is a shift in the power relationship between teacher and taught, so that more of each is likely to enter the pedagogical relationship. Furthermore, as content becomes more open to negotiation there is a shift from the surface to the deep structure of knowledge (Bernstein, 1971). Therefore, with the older children, 9 to 11 year age range, greater emphasis can be placed on the cognitive features of playing games. This would mean a move away from the didactic-reception learning so often seen, towards self-regulating or group learning. This change may be described using Bernstein's rather ambiguous concept of framing:

> the degree of control teacher and pupil possess over the selection, organization, pacing and timing of the knowledge transmitted and received in the pedagogical relationship. (p. 43)

Spontaneous Interest

It has been argued that skill teaching lays the foundation for future learning. However, if these foundations are laid without the spontaneous interest of the child being taken into account they might well be unsound. The teacher should be the external trigger by offering activities calculated to be interesting to the child.

If games teaching is to become an educationally viable proposition I submit that the spontaneous interest of the child should be linked with discovery methods of learning. By encouraging the children to 'see what they are looking at' we are teaching the skill of observation. If we then extend this to a search for patterns in the observation we are at the lowest level of classification, and it is at this point that discovery methods assume an importance. By and large what is meant here by 'discovery' is that children see for themselves the patterns that are present. The finding out of the reasons for such patterns comes much later.

The grasp of game patterns and recognizing causes of actions and the ability to subsume one's own interests in the interests of the team or group as a whole are attributes not usually associated with primary school children. Although they will normally work quite happily together, cooperation in the form of 'team work' is largely outside their behavioural scope. Collaboration within a team at this age often means six individuals rather than one team of six, for the role-play expected of them is often not fully understood. Junior children tend to prefer to keep score as a measure of their personal skill, and for enjoyment of the activity, rather than for comparison with other children.

Ideally, children should be taking part because their interest has been triggered, and should continue to do so just as long as they remain interested. By their words and deeds they will indicate if the excitement remains or is on the wane. It is, therefore, very important that they be encouraged and helped to convey freely this interest and excitement — the feeling of fun should always be present and part of the teacher's remit is to make the activity fun and an enjoyable experience. One might go even further and argue that at the primary stage there should be no question of teaching specialist techniques for major games, like soccer and netball skills in curriculum time but that these should be taught as extra-curricular activities.

Cooperative Games

Terry Orlick (1979) looks at the spontaneous interests of the child from a totally different angle. He is concerned with the quality of children's lives and the quality of children's games. He argues that genuine cooperative games with no losers are extremely rare in the western world. In this view games should be about challenge, stimulation, self-validation, success and sheer fun.

His thesis starts from the factory model of society, stating that society has become production minded, machine orientated and over-specialized, resulting in the 'industrialization' of children's games. They have become rigid, judgmental, highly organized and excessively goal orientated. There is no freedom from the pressure of evaluation and the psychological distress of disapproval. He goes on to say that because children's games are now designed for elimination they guarantee failure and rejection for the many, and by squeezing the most out of each individual there is little, if any, room for 'plain old fun'? By conditioning children to the importance of winning leads to labels like 'failure', 'rejects' and 'duffers', for the vast majority.

I'm No Good at Games

One of Orlick's main arguments is that failure often leads children to avoid games and competition, and to withdraw from situations whenever possible. Failure at games may also 'teach' children totally unjustifiable 'bad things' about themselves. So children nurtured on cooperation, acceptance and success, according to Orlick, have a much better chance of developing strong self-concepts, just as children nurtured on balanced diets have a greater chance of developing strong healthy bodies.

Self-esteem

When bodies and minds are being formed shouldn't we give the child a firm base from which to start? Won't this enable him/her to meet and cope better with a variety of situations later in life? Children spend a lot of time playing during their developmental years and if this play is marred by exposure to failure and rejection then negative self-perceptions are likely to occur. Hyland, researching in the USA, found that junior school children who opted out of physical education had a lower self-esteem and lower perceptions of sports ability and more negative perceptions about their bodies than their peers who elected to take physical education.

Teaching Strategies

These, and similar findings, emphasize the need to develop a games teaching strategy where all participants are accepted on their own terms and can at least experience a modicum of success. A strategy is needed which enables children to learn from their mistakes without feeling shame, which will help build self-esteem and develop coping strategies. In creating one's own games it is the framework and structure of the game which is so important. The overall game environment must provide the opportunity for decision making and choice between alternatives, for the game depends upon the creative power of the children, within a few simple guidelines. This involves verbal interaction in the sharing and refining of ideas, and in cooperation and working together.

In order to evaluate the degree of success of any such programme the teacher must *watch* the children, *listen* to their discussions, *ask* questions, all in as informal and unobtrusive a way as possible. For example, ask questions to ascertain a child's understanding of how the game is played, the level of involvement of themselves and everybody else and the level of cooperation, of helping and sharing. Are they being considerate to others and, most important of all, are they having fun? If not, why not, and is it a problem that possibly the teacher can help with the solution? Is the level of skill challenging enough to keep the game exciting or is boredom creeping in?

Recent Research

Over the past two years my own researches at secondary school level have tended to support the findings of Thorpe and Bunker, Almond and Spackman. I did find that the children were able to recognize features and skills common to all games, and that the cognitive elements when planning games lessons could be emphasized by the teacher. However, with junior school children, where most of my work was concentrated, I could not find any empirical evidence to support such findings. I found that the junior children were fairly barren of new ideas when involved in a games-making situation. The Thorpe and Bunker model based on a game form was difficult to follow. The game form produced often showed little potential for development, it broke down for many reasons other than lack of skill, the decision making element was often simply the result of one child 'deciding' what was going to happen, (although the decision makers did change roles), and generally the cyclic nature of the model could not be followed.

However, if the children did not show a deeper understanding of the underlying principles of games, (such as creating and denying space), or appeared to lack a certain degree of creativity and inventiveness, there is no doubt in my mind that they were more actively engaged in their games lessons. Is this not a more desirable outcome? By abandoning, in the preparation of our research lessons, such details as lesson material, activity, teaching points, organization, technique and method, and concentrating upon lesson objectives and evaluations emphasis was put upon the child and his/her learning, and so the lessons were very much child centred. We wanted to avoid falling into the trap of 'teaching a lesson' by being too technically prepared, for we were very conscious that we must 'teach the child'.

Any teacher with a sound knowledge of the basic disciplines of education should be able to further the progress of his/her pupils towards ends which are largely pre-determined. He/she must be able to analyze a situation, select appropriate aims and objectives, devise related learning opportunities and assess the progress of the children. Teachers are individuals and apply their skills and individuality to the needs of the children, consciously or unconsciously. Children are also individuals and in an ideal world individual needs, attainments, potentialities and interests would be catered for. But the world of schooling is rarely ideal and so often its harsh realities demand practicalities in which individual curricula become extremely rare, especially in the physical education curriculum.

In traditional games teaching, children are often presented with a skill-based lesson. A few of the children will have already acquired the skill, many of the children will never be able to master the skill, and the rest will learn an isolated skill out of context. Games through understanding or games making is therefore an attempt at individualized learning and through the cooperative elements and socializing factors aims at putting the child at the centre of the educational process. The aim is to devise learning opportunities which hopefully will maximize the learning of all the children taking part. Children should be encouraged to solve problems, make decisions and choices, and by the nature of the activity they engage in justify their decisions and choices. They should be given appropriate learning opportunities to develop the skills necessary to make wise and sensible decisions, and to reflect upon the implications of the decisions they make.

There is a tradition in this country that 'anybody can teach games',

Figure 5.1: A model for teaching games

The following model outlines the procedure, step by step, whereby the teacher helps the child to achieve a new level of skilful performance. While absolute levels of performance will vary, each and every child is able to participate in decision making based upon tactical awareness thereby retaining an interest and involvement in the game.

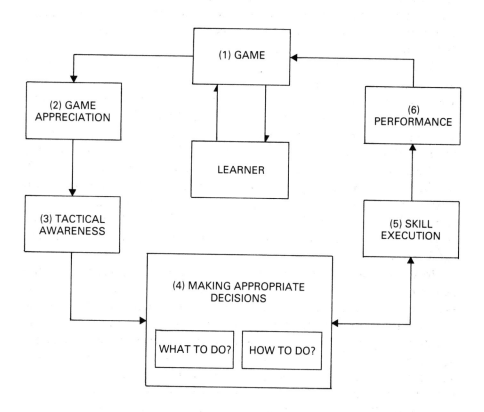

and many teachers, because they have little idea how to develop a major game, and fearing that others might question that they are teaching anything at all, spend a lot of time on the teaching of isolated skills, often with fairly barren results. However, my research suggests that in a games making programme it is the decision-making process which should be of paramount importance, for without the ability to select appropriate responses a pupil's skill and technique can be rendered quite ineffectual. Brian Sutton-Smith argued that learning which occurs in play is most useful when the future is characterized by uncertainty and where there is a need for a person to be flexible and have a wide repertoire of responses available.

So an attempt was made in my own research programme (see Asquith 1987) to evaluate the consequences of teaching a series of lessons without emphasizing the skill element. The game was the focus of each lesson and oppportunities were presented to the children to make rules, solve problems, use skill and last, but by no means least, encourage everybody to take a full and active part. Piaget (1951) said that the real value of play is the opportunity it affords children to alter reality so that it corresponds with their view of the world. This was supported by Erickson (1963) when he emphasized that individual experimentation and exploration were means by which children learned to cope with experience and reality. Games making does provide plenty of action and personal involvement, of interpersonal dialogue and numerous opportunities to organize time, space and activity.

Any programme involving such radical changes in teaching strategies and child expectancy would possibly benefit by its introduction early in the child's school life before stereotyped responses are allowed to develop. If games making, often started as individual activities at infant level, were continued and developed into group and team activities throughout the junior school a lot of time would be saved in re-learning new working methods, and responses.

In our first ten weeks of 'games making' we had looked to the following aspects:

1 Safety, and areas of play
2 Use of space and possession
3 Rule making and methods of scoring
4 Playing 'fair' and accepting rules

The children appeared to be so conditioned into being told exactly what to do in a games lesson that they found the freedom involved in games-making difficult to come to terms with. The richness of innovation, experimentation, experiential learning etc, so frequently discussed in educational writings, took a long time to appear. Initially the children were noisy and appeared barren of ideas, derivations of netball or soccer dominated the invasion type game lesson. However, as the term progressed ideas did start to come through but it was a long hard process. Initially much teacher intervention was required to keep any form of game moving and often it was difficult to record any real development.

As the research programme progressed, the teacher and I noticed a change in attitude amongst the children. Many of the problems encountered in the first term, i.e. discipline, listening skills and obedience to instructions, became less obvious as the children took a more active part in the lessons. How much part maturation played in this process it was difficult to assess.

Another interesting feature of the programme was the change that occurred in the assessment provided by the pupils as they watched other children at work. The critiques gradually 'moved' from being overly negative to being positively constructive. It appeared that once the children really understood what was being asked of them, then they tended to become quite instructive and helpful. Initially they seemed to be measuring observed actions against a yardstick of major games and comparing one person's actions with another. Once they realized that each game was different, that the skills involved were slightly different, then they changed their criticisms from generalities to particulars, and in so doing became much more positive. If one is to understand games one must be tactically aware and be able to make decisions. By teaching the children skills of observation, we felt that they gradually became able to analyze what was happening and comment on how and what peer group members were doing.

The skill development of the children in such basic areas as throwing, catching, hitting and collecting did not appear to have suffered by the non-skill teaching emphasis in the innovatory teaching programme. Although skill teaching was not given the prominence that it receives in more traditional games teaching nonetheless skills were still taught. For example, if the children were devising a game involving catching and it was beyond the skill level of the group then intervention was necessary and basic techniques of particular skills were taught.

It might well be that at times the whole class works on some aspect of skill that the teacher thinks the children will benefit from. But the skill element comes from an observed need rather than a superimposed dictum. Skills must be taught if progress cannot be made without them, and the development of the game is prevented.

Counter-arguments

Over the past few years schemes have been introduced to promote specific games. Often such schemes are in the form of mini-games, (for example, short tennis, mini-hockey), and are based upon a skill learning by playing approach. Nevertheless they are still based on techniques and specific skills. A games-making approach goes even further for the children can enjoy their sport without being great technicians of specific skills.

By contrast one must acknowledge the viewpoint expressed by a large number of teachers and coaches. Concern is expressed over the movement in physical education towards experiential learning. It is felt that a dramatic shift in the physical education curriculum from the narrow 'major games' type activity to a much broader 'option' type curriculum is not always in the best interests of the children. It is argued that the children are not being given the vocabulary of skills upon which to build any real game form or expertise in specific areas. Games teaching is sometimes compared with reading and writing and the need to master basic skills before sentences, paragraphs, chapters and stories can be read or written.

Here we have two competing ideologies which teachers have to confront routinely in everyday practice. It may be the case that one has to choose between these ideologies. If one is to achieve 'excellence' in sport then it would seem appropriate to dedicate oneself completely to the pursuit of these goals and practices which are necessary in its attainment. Teachers have to decide towards which end of the spectrum children will gain most educational benefit.

Broad Based Curriculum	Narrow Games Curriculum
Games-making	Games Coaching
Non-Competitive	Centres of Excellence
Danger: We may rob the child of his/her *heritage.*	*Danger:* We may rob the child of his/her *childhood.*

Primary school teachers need to enter this debate and decide their position within this teaching continuum. They will need to be aware of 'where games are going' as they are the ones responsible for laying the foundations.

Games-making is not an easy approach to teaching games in the primary school. It is clear that much time will be spent on discussing strategies and methods, contents and responses, and generally wrestling with the many problems presented in an attempt at putting more of the responsibility for learning into the hands of the children. In asking for better games teaching then teachers in the primary sector must be better trained in the art of Physical Education. Teaching games through understanding, even more than a skill based programme, requires more resources, time, effort, equipment, and above all else the knowledge and a principle of commitment to child-centred education. There is no one prescriptive method of games teaching in this form. So much will depend upon parental and peer influence, the age and abilities of the children involved and the length of time spent on games-making. However, the effort might well be worthwhile for Devereaux (1976) talked about the 'impoverishment' of play and informal games by the growth of organized sport. And it might well be that this 'impoverish-ment' is one of the major obstacles to any rapid development in a games-making programme.

Possibly teachers might become more reflective about what they are doing and more aware of the factors which influence their behaviour. They might benefit from a focusing of attention on other aspects of 'school life' and utilizing the 'child culture', events and actions which can, and do influence both teacher's and pupil's performance, approach and conduct during lessons.

It may be the case that games-making or teaching games through understanding will not survive as an isolated philosophy and that it will need to be part of a broader and possibly richer physical education curriculum. Games-making interspersed with minor games and games developed from the 'child culture' may present a much more balanced diet on which to base the games curriculum.

At the moment, I have argued, the balance is wrong. Games teaching in most schools is based on specific skills derived from adult games, and often at primary level not yet part of the 'child culture'. Therefore, I suggest that primary school teachers should develop their games teach-ing on a games making approach, possibly based on street type games with minor games, (*not* mini-games), such as continuous rounders, longball and king ball, helping form a basis for creative and inventive work from the children.

It could well be that the main value for primary education, as far as games playing is concerned, is that this approach keeps the children's minds open and active until they are physically and mentally ready for a more systematic approach. Ultimately an increase in participation with more creativity and spontaneous activity might well bring more children and young people to see the benefits that can be accrued from playing games.

What we can do as teachers is to stimulate interest and curiosity in the children, improve our practice and understanding of teaching, and challenge traditional thinking about games teaching. Then we might start the slow progress of change to new practices and new understanding.

References

ALMOND, L. (1983) 'Games making', *Bulletin of Physical Education*, 19, 1, spring (1987).

ASQUITH, A. (1987) *'An Investigation into games teaching in the primary school'*, unpublished dissertation, University of Southampton.

BENNETT, N. *et al.* (1984) *The Quality of Pupil Learning Experiences*, London, Erlbaum.

BERNSTEIN, B. (1971) *Distribution of Power and Principles of Social Control.* London, Routledge & Kegan Paul.

DEVEREAUX (1976) in Coakley, J.J. (1980) 'Play, Games and Sport: Developmental Implications for Young People', *Journal of Sports Behaviour*, 3, 3.

ERICKSON (1963) in Coakley, J.J. *op. cit.*

MAULDON, E. and REDFERN, H.B. (1981) *Games Teaching. An Approach for the Primary School*, (2nd edn) Plymouth, Macdonald, Evans.

ORLICK, T. (1979) *The Co-operative Games and Sports Book: Challenge without Competition*, New York, Writers and Readers.

PIAGET (1951) in Coakley, J.J. *op. cit.*

RICHARDS, C. (1985) *The Study of Primary Education. A Source Book. Vol 2*, Lewes, Falmer Press.

SPACKMAN, L. (Ed) (1983) *Teaching Games for Understanding*, Cheltenham, Curriculum Development Centre, The College of St Paul and St Mary.

TAWNEY, R.H. (1961) *The Acquisitive Society*, London, Fontana Library.

THORPE, R. and BUNKER, D. (1986) *Landmarks on our way to Teaching Games for Understanding*, London, City Publisher.

Part B:
The Child

Chapter 6:
Some Aspects of the Exercise Physiology of Children

Craig Sharp

As exercise and sport become more popular, young children are becoming increasingly involved in intensive training, in addition to being encouraged to take regular exercise. I have, for example, been associated with the England Under-10 Boys Squash Squad, and there are many other instances of youth sport, apart from the traditional early-recruiting sports of swimming and gymnastics. Children differ from adults in some of their responses to hard physical activity. Children are not simply 'little adults' physiologically, and here I shall discuss important areas of difference, both qualitative and quantitative.

Size

Children do not grow at an even rate. In particular, there is an 'adolescent growth spurt' which carries them through puberty, and is a time of very marked growth with up to six inches (fifteen cms) over two years being common. The spurt occurs about two years earlier in girls than in boys. It commonly begins between the ages of 10–12 years in girls and 12–14 years in boys, and stretches over about two years in each case. Thus, there is a stage when many girls will be bigger, heavier and possibly stronger than boys of the same age. Also, children of the same sex and age may be at very different stages in their growth, and this has implications for age-group sport. Some early-maturing youngsters may give up the unequal struggle and drop out of sport altogether.

Bones

Before the growth spurt, boys and girls are much the same in skeletal terms. After their respective spurts, however, the girls end up with a broader pelvis and hips, and the boys come to have relatively broader shoulders and longer arms. Their broader hips are one reason why some girls tend to throw out their heels when they run. Some girls may also develop a pronounced 'carrying' or valgus angle in their arms, which may cause some interference with throwing.

Long bones grow from epiphyseal plates of cartilage near each end. These plates may be damaged by severe overload stress in occasional high performance youthful competitors. This may lead to cessation of long bone growth altogether, or it may lead to distortion producing various degrees of valgus or varus angle. In the case of the arm, 80 per cent of the growth of the humerus occurs in the proximal part of that bone, that is at the shoulder end. In the case of the forearm, 75 per cent of bone growth occurs in the distal part of the radius and 80 per cent in the distal part of the ulnar, that is, nearer the wrist. Thus, in the arm overall, only about 20 per cent of the growth in length of three long bones occurs around the elbow. Hence, elbow injuries to the growing child in this sense may not be so damaging as in the case of equivalent injuries to the leg. In the leg, the growth situation is virtually the reverse of the arm. Here 70 per cent of the growth of the femur occurs at the distal or knee end, while 60 per cent and 55 per cent respectively of the growth in length of the tibia and fibula occur at the proximal or knee end. Thus, damage to the epiphyseal plates in the knee area is relatively more serious than those in the upper and lower part of the leg. The various doping agents in the category of anabolic steroids, if used in children before the epiphyseal plates have calcified, may also cause damage and premature calcification of the plates and so lead to stunting or distortion of growth.

Various other bony projections or epiphyses fuse together to form the whole mature bone throughout the teens. Repetition stress, as may happen in sport or dance, may affect this process and Grisogono (1985) has noted the frequency of heel pain in those up to 12-years-old (Sever's Disease), knee pain in up to 16-year-olds (Osgood Schlatter's) and back pain (Scheurman's Disease) in those up to 20 years of age.

Body Fat

During childhood, girls have only slightly more fat than boys. For example, at the age of 8 a girl may have 18 per cent and a boy 16 per cent body fat. During the growth spurt, the girls tend to put on fat, up to about 25 per cent at 17, while the boys tend to lose it, going down to 12 per cent to 14 per cent at the same age. This difference may well help the girls in swimming (buoyancy, streamlining) and in keeping warmer under cold conditions — and, of course, it is largely responsible for the changing shape of the female adolescent, a change which may bring with it alterations in the centre of gravity in the body and in limb segments which may influence some high-skill sports, such as gymnastics, diving and trampolining.

Contrary to popular belief, fat children are often not greedy in terms of excess calorie intake. For example, Johnson, *et al.* (1956) have shown that overweight adolescent girls tend to have a much lower calorie turnover than their normal weight controls. Similarly, Rose and Mayer (1968) have shown that the percentage body fat of six-month infants is positively related to lack of activity rather than calorie intake. Lack of exercise or activity is extremely important in adolescent obesity. With sports groups, of course, one has always to bear in mind the possibility of anorexia nervosa in some female adolescents. In many sports relatively low body fat is obviously desirable, but with the vulnerable female age-groups I indicate that a 'reasonable' level of body fat is necessary, and I tend to place that level at least around 18 per cent. In my experience, between 16 per cent and 18 per cent is the threshold body fat value in the young woman below which she may well temporarily stop menstruating. Such amenorrhoea may be associated with a degree of osteoporosis, or calcium loss from bones, which may in turn be associated with stress fractures. Thus one can make out a good case for the teenage to early 20s sportswoman not to get too low in body fat, or in body weight or indeed not to have less than four menstrual periods per year.

Increases in body fat occur because of increases in fat cell size, or in the number of such fat cells, or both. Fat cells appear to increase in number until early adolescence, after which increases in body fat occur mainly by increasing cell size. It may be possible to affect the development of fat cells during the growth of the child by means of diet (cutting down on sweets and 'junk food'), physical activity and exercise. Fat children occur in both sexes, and 80 per cent of them go on to be fat adults. As mentioned, lack of exercise is a very important factor in obesity, and obese children take much less exercise even when they are active. Obese children require a higher oxygen uptake to do a given task, yet their maximal oxygen uptake is often lower than that of leaner children, so activity seems harder for them (Boileau, *et al.* 1985).

Children in general possess more of the heat-producing tissue known as 'brown fat' which diminishes as they get older. Brown fat *may* have a weight-regulating function, acting as a 'ponderostat', and it *may* be that obese children are born with relatively less of it.

Heart and Lungs

Maximal adult heart rates for both sexes are about 200 per minute at 20 years old. Children's rates can go higher, up to 215 or more, but decline once physical maturity has been reached. This high rate is presumably to compensate for their relatively smaller hearts. At relatively equal exercise loads, a child's heart may well beat at twenty per minute more than an adult, and at lower blood pressure.

It has been suggested (for example, Morganroth, *et al.* 1975) that high levels of isotonic exercise in childhood (swimming, running, hockey, lacrosse, squash, football) would produce large hearts with relatively unthickened walls whereas 'strength' sports (rowing, canoeing, weight-training, gymnastics) would produce smaller hearts with relatively much thicker walls. Speculation has centred on whether such thicker-walled hearts might not lead to higher increases in blood pressure in later life. However, Dr Len Shapiro, among others, has indicated that considerable doubt exists regarding such a dichotomy in the cardiac response to training.

Children have much higher respiratory rates than adults during exercise, taking shorter and shallower breaths; for example, where an adult might take forty breaths per minute, a child might take sixty. The 6-year-old child may need to breathe thirty-eight litres of air to gain one litre of oxygen during maximal exercise, whereas the 18-year-old needs only twenty-eight litres, (Bar-Or, 1983). This is not harmful, but it is wasteful of energy and body water (and, en masse, may be one cause of the 'contagious hysterias' of children — a response to the feeling induced by blowing off too much carbon dioxide). Such 'hyperventilation hypocapnia' may also lead to cramp-like contractions of hands and feet, one cure for which is to breathe in and out of a medium-sized paper bag for periods of around ten seconds at a time.

Aerobic Power

This term refers to the amount of oxygen the body can use in a given time. The more oxygen that is used, the more energy is generated by muscle. Between 5 and 10 years of age aerobic power is much the same in both sexes. Due to their earlier growth spurts some girls may go ahead, but from about 14 onwards they tend not to improve on a volume-of-oxygen-per-weight basis (mainly because of the marked increase in body fat percentage), whereas boys continue to improve until 18. Children are 'wasteful' of energy, probably for various biomechanical and biochemical (lower stores of muscle glycogen, lower concentrations of appropriate muscle enzymes) reasons. For example, the oxygen costs of walking and running in children are higher than in adults. The energy cost of treadmill walking decreases from, for example, $47ml.O_2/kg/min$ at 6 years old down to 38ml at 17 (boys at 10 km/hr-1; Astrand, 1952) and there are similar differences in uphill walking (Skinner, *et al.* 1971). For cycling, the energy costs are much closer for younger and older children; the cycle seems to make the younger children relatively more efficient.

Thus, older children are higher in 'aerobic power' than younger children, but all children gain a higher proportion of their energy from aerobic than anaerobic sources, compared to adults.

Anaerobic Power

The ability of children to perform anaerobic activities is distinctly lower than that of adolescents who in turn are lower in this ability than adults. Anaerobic activities may be taken to include those which are very intense and last up to a minute, such as the sprint swims and runs, and the jumps and throws, or those games such as netball, lacross, gaelic football, hurling, football, badminton and squash where frequent bursts of activity are required (as they are to an even greater extent in artistic and rhythmic gymnastics, karate, akido, judo, boxing and wrestling).

Even when normalized for body-weight differences, the anaerobic energy produced by an 8-year-old is only 70 per cent of that produced by an 11-year-old, which in turn is less than that of a 14-year-old (Kurowski, 1977). The child's muscle has less glycogen, and a much lower rate of utilisation of glycogen, and it has less creatine-phosphate, the anaerobic energy store. Eriksson (1971) among others, has shown that children's muscle produces very much less lactic acid than that of the adult. Children incur less of an oxygen deficit at the beginning of exercise (Macek and Vavra, 1980) which implies that they gain their 'second wind' quicker than adults. Also, their capacity for acquiring an 'oxygen debt' (post-exercise recovery oxygen) is less than that of adults and their 'anaerobic threshold' (the point at which they eventually do go anaerobic) is much higher. This is a major reason why many children seem able to be constantly active.

The implications of this are that children are much more aerobic than adults, so ideally their activity should be longer, rather than shorter. They are metabolically more at home running longer distances (800 and 1500 metres) than 50 to 200 metres; in fact, they are well adapted to relatively long periods (with rest intervals) of moderate physical activity. Nevertheless, as Eriksson, et al. (1971) has shown with boys from 11 to 15 years, all their anaerobic parameters may be increased with training.

Metabolic Specialists

Mature adults, of either sex, tend to fall into three activity groups: those who are good at vigorous short exercise (anaerobic); those who are good at the 'long' activities (aerobic ones, such as cycle-touring, marathons, long swims and fell-walking); and a third group who can do both but neither particularly well. In other words, adults tend to specialize, metabolically speaking. They do not have much control over this as it is to a considerable extent due to the genetic make-up of their muscle in terms of fast and slow fibre types. Young children, say up to 10 (girls) and 12 (boys), are very much less specialized in this way; the ones who can run far can usually run fast as well, but this gradually changes as they get older. Basic muscle cell patterns are decided from birth but the patterns do not become fully effective until the time between puberty and full maturity.

Strength

For adults, at least part of the process of becoming stronger is the ability of the central nervous system to 'learn' to recruit a higher percentage of its individual fibres into relatively simultaneous contraction. In children, this ability seems to be less pronounced. When they gain strength it is mainly due to hypertrophy of the muscle cells. Boys tend to have fairly large increases in strength after puberty, when the anabolic effect of their testicular hormones triggers hypertrophy on an already increasing muscle mass. Girls do not tend to have such marked pubertal effect (although they do produce some anabolic androgens from their adrenal glands, and some of their ovarian hormone has an anabolic effect). Indeed, girls tend to have a more gradual rise in strength from a younger age and some workers believe that their muscle is more sensitive to the effects of growth hormone, which is present throughout childhood. This has led to claims that girls are more responsive to strength-training before puberty than are boys. In both sexes one should beware of too heavy weight-training until full bone growth has been achieved, as discussed above.

Davies (1985) has found that the strength of human muscle is 33 Newtons/cm2 for children and young adults, irrespective of age and sex — very similar to other mammalian muscle.

Heat Balance

Children expend more chemical energy per kilogram of body weight than do adults, so they produce more body heat, but for various reasons it may be harder for them to disperse the heat from the skin. The sweating apparatus is developed by the age of 3, but even so children sweat less than adults — in the case of boys a lot less, as women tend to sweat less than men by considerable amounts. Twelve-year-old boys may sweat 400–500ml per square metre of body surface per hour, compared to a man's rate of 700–800ml (Araki, *et al*, 1979). There are actually more sweat glands in a given area of children's skin, but they seem to produce nearly three times less sweat per gland. Also, children tend to have higher skin temperature, which hinders the flow of heat from the body core to the periphery because the internal heat gradient is less. If the environmental temperature is greater than body temperature (or if exposed to too much direct sun), children run into overheating problems for another reason — connected with their greater surface area.

In general, for the same shape, the smaller an object is, the bigger is its surface area relative to its weight. A young adult, 177cms tall and weighing 64kg, will have a surface area of 1.80 square metres. An 8-year-old, 128cms tall and weighing 25kg will have a surface area of 0.95 square metres. Thus the young child has 36 per cent more skin surface for his or her weight. In too hot an environment, that can lead to a faster rate of heating. Children can 'heat acclimatize', but may take up to three times as long as adults to do so.

In too cold an environment — for example, during swimming, especially outdoors, the greater skin area of the child can lead to overcooling and hypothermia much sooner than in adults. Also, young children have less insulating fat immediately under their skins, compared to adults of both sexes. In work by Sloan and Keatinge with age groups from 8 to 19 years old, the subjects were asked to swim at a speed that represented an increase of five times their resting rate of metabolism, for thirty minutes in a pool at 20°C. The older age groups completed the swim without difficulty, but the younger children showed distress and had to be taken from the water in around eighteen to twenty minutes, when their body temperatures were found to have dropped by 2–3°C. Municipal and other pools are usually maintained at 25°C or above, but many outdoor swimming situations occur at temperatures of 20°C or much lower. This provides a potential risk, especially for the very keen, lean, small-sized swimmer, who is often reluctant to leave the water. Euphoria, excitability and disorientation are warning signs of hypothermia in such situations.

Voluntary Dehydration

With their ability to be physically active for very long periods of time and with their very high breathing rates (and ventilatory equivalents) —

both leading to losses of body fluid — children quite easily become relatively dehydrated. This is because, although they become thirsty and drink, tests have shown that they only drink about two-thirds of what they lose — hence the term 'voluntary dehydration'. It will tend to happen gradually on long hot days, and will tend to aggravate any other heat-loss problem such as vigorous exercise. This is a recognized condition in some warmer countries known as 'thirst-fever'. The 'fever', or raised body temperature, is not due to any infection, but is simply a combination of too long overheating and too little fluid, and disappears on the child being adequately rehydrated.

For endurance sport over an hour or more, the liquid and electrolyte replacement drink recommended by Bar-Or (1983, p 281) is water containing up to 0.3g/litre of sodium chloride, up to 0.28g/litre of potassium chloride and up to 25g/litre of sugar. This takes into account the relatively low salt content of children's sweat.

Obese children are at a greater risk in the heat (less in the cold!), and as they tend to sweat more than normal, can be at greater risk from dehydration. After one hour walking at 4.8km hr-1 on a 5 per cent incline in dry heat at 40–42°C (25 per cent relative humidity), 9–12-year-old boys classed as 'obese' had rectal temperatures 0.5°C higher than 'lean' controls and heart rate thirty-five beats per minute higher (Haymes, *et al.* 1975).

Exercise Perception

There are various simple methods whereby a level of exertion may be rated in terms of its relative degree of hardship. On this basis, exercise at equivalent levels is perceived as much easier by children than adolescents, and hardest by adults, (Bar-Or, 1977). Also, partly because of their more aerobic metabolism, there is a much faster rate of recovery in young subjects. After a maximum aerobic test in the laboratory it may be several hours before adults can be persuaded into a further test. Yet many children want to repeat the test well within the hour, to see if they can do better! The habitual high levels of activity of children may result from their not perceiving it as particularly strenuous; adults may prefer their more sedentary style just because they do perceive exercise as particularly fatiguing.

The lesson for sport is that in working with youthful squads, the coach should call for short breaks with drinks every twenty minutes or so. This is to act as a check against dehydration, overheating and simple exhaustion.

Conclusion

It is both completely natural and important that children should indulge in considerable physical activity. However, they are not simply small adults, and some of the ways in which they differ from adults are discussed above. The safest course is to let children set their own levels of activity for the most part. Problems arise when children are made to conform to an adult concept of sport, training and exercise.

References

ARAKI, T., TODA, Y., MATSUSHITA, K. and TSUJINO, A. (1979) 'Age differences in sweating during muscular exercise', *Japanese Journal of Physical Fitness and Sports Medicine*, 28, pp 239–48.

ASTRAND, P.-O. (1952) *Experimental Studies of the Physical Working Capacity in Relation to Sex and Age*, Copenhagen, Munksgaard.

BAR-OR, O. (1977) 'Age-related changes in exercise perception' in BORG, G. (Ed) *Physical Work and Effort*, Oxford, Pergamon Press, pp 255–66.

BAR-OR, O. (1983) *Pediatric Sports Medicine*, New York, Springer-Verlag.

BOILEAU, R.A., LOHMAN, T.G. and SLAUGHTER, H. (1985) 'Exercise and body composition of children and youth', *Scandinavian Journal of Sports Science*, 7.1, pp 17–27.

DAVIES, C.T.M. (1985) 'Strength and mechanical properties of muscle in children and young adults', *Scandinavian Journal of Sports Science*, 7.1, pp 11–15.

ERIKSSON, B.O., KARLSSON, J. and SALTIN, B. (1971) 'Muscle metabolites during exercise in pubertal boys'. *Acta Paediatrica Scandinavica*, Supplement, 217, pp 154–7.

GRISOGONO, V. (1985) 'Injury and the role of the physiotherapist', *Coaching Focus*, 2, autumn, pp 5–6.

HAYMES, E.M., McCORMICK, R.J. and BUSKIRK, E.R. (1975) 'Heat tolerance of exercising lean and heavy pubertal boys', *Journal of Applied Physiology*, 39, pp 457–61.

JOHNSON, M.L., BURKE, B.S. and MAYER, J. (1956) 'Relative importance of inactivity and overeating in the energy balance of obese high school girls', *American Journal of Clinical Nutrition*, 4, pp 37–44.

KUROWSKI, T.T. (1977) 'Anaerobic power of children from age 9 through 15 years', MSc thesis, Florida State University (*quoted in* BAR-OR, O. 1983).

MACEK, M. and VAVRA, J. (1980) 'The adjustments of oxygen uptake at the onset of exercise: A comparison between pre-pubertal boys and young adults'. *International Journal of Sports Medicine*, 1, pp 75–7.

MORGANROTH, J., MARON, B.J., HENRY, W.L. and EPSTEIN, E.E. (1975) 'Comparative left ventricular dimensions in trained athletes, *Annals of International Medicine*, 82, pp 521–4.

ROSE, H.E. and MAYER, J. (1968) 'Activity, calorie intake, fat storage and the energy balance of infants', *Paediatrics*, 41, pp. 18–28.

SHAPIRO, L. (cardiologist, National Heart Hospital, London) — personal communication, 1986.

SKINNER, J.S., BAR-OR, O. and BERGSTEINOVA, V. (1971) 'Comparison of continuous and intermittent tests for determining maximum oxygen intake of children', *Acta Paediatric Scandinovica*, Supplement, 217, pp 24–8.

SLOAN, R.E.G. and KEATINGE, W.R. (1973) 'Cooling rates of young people swimming in cold water'. *Journal of Applied Physiology*, 35, pp 371–5.

General Reading

An excellent book from which I have drawn much data for this chapter is:
BAR-OR, O. (1983) *Pediatric Sports Medicine*. New York, Springer-Verlag. Three chapters are especially relevant: chapter 1, 'Physiological responses of the healthy child' (pp 1–65); chapter 6, 'Nutritional diseases' (pp 192–226), covering anorexia nervosa and obesity very well; chapter 9 (pp 259–99) 'Climate and the exercising child', with very good guidelines for the conduct of sports events in the heat.

Also worth reading selectively is the collection of articles published as:
ILMARINEN, J. and VLMAKI, I. (Eds) (1984) *Children and Sport*, New York, Springer-Verlag.

Chapter 7:
The Child in the Teaching-learning Process

Rosie Connell

In 1976 Wade commented that much of the available literature on children's motor skill development was by nature descriptive, i.e. it outlined in detail the performance of children of various ages on a large variety of motor activities. While it described when children can achieve certain levels of performance it failed to explain why or how they develop skills. The move from a product to a process approach, favoured by Connell (1984) and Keogh and Sugden (1985) has been slow in coming, and may be one reason for the fact that, in physical education, the task or sporting skill rather than the learner, has frequently been given primary importance by the teacher. Specification of the ideal technique, breaking down the skill into its component parts, recognition of its spatial, temporal and force characteristics have been seen as central for the learning/teaching process. It might reasonably be asked, 'Where is the learner in motor learning?'

This chapter seeks to place the learner very firmly in the forefront of the learning process and focuses primarily on the cognitive abilities and affective characteristics which the child brings to the learning situation.

Clearly learning outcomes are the result of interactions between the learner, task and teacher, before, during and after the period of practice. The interactive model presented in figure 7.1 forms the framework for this enquiry into how children learn motor skills, and from it will arise guidelines for teachers.

Focusing on the learner rather than the task means that the first stage is for the teacher to assess the child's entry characteristics i.e. his/her

Figure 7.1: Interactions in the learning/teaching process

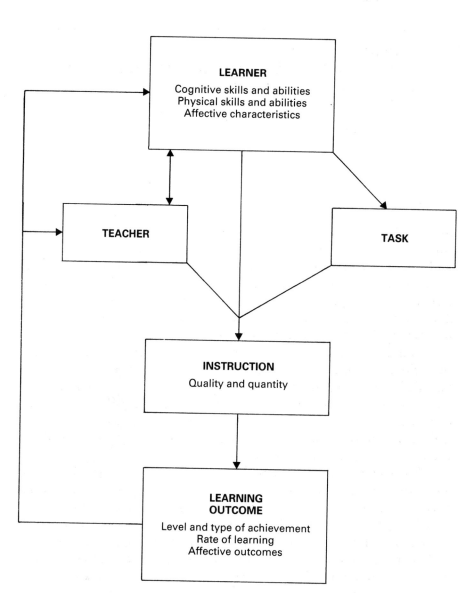

physical, cognitive and affective skills and abilities. Subsequently, s/he should analyze the task in terms of its novelty, complexity and specific physical, mental and emotional demands and only then, select an appropriate teaching method.

Careful monitoring of the child's response provides the basis for modification of manner of presentation and speed of progression.

Learner Entry Characteristics

Physical Skills and Abilities

These may be grouped into three categories: anthropometric and physical fitness characteristics, psychomotor abilities and the level and range of physical skills previously developed.

The former refers to such attributes as height, limb length, strength-to-weight ratio, flexibility, speed and endurance. The relevance of these attributes will clearly be dependent on the task, for example, while height may be helpful to children playing aerial passing games, strength-to-weight ratio will be more important in tasks demanding speed. While these attributes may influence motor performance, their effect on learning is chiefly mediated by the feelings of success or failure which the child experiences as a result of initial performance. Clearly the teacher should do all in his/her power to structure the task in a way in which all children can achieve at their own level and are not disadvantaged by physical factors during skill learning.

Psychomotor abilities include speed of reactions, coordination, the ability to control the rate of movement, and manual dexterity. While these abilities may be determined in part genetically, practice has an improving effect. Again their direct influence is on performance rather than learning. However, the child with impoverished psychomotor abilities will be slow in developing expertise and be prone to self-concept, confidence and motivation problems.

According to Schmidt who developed the schema theory of motor learning in 1975, it is not only the range of different skills, for example, footwork, interception, striking skills which is important, but also the variability of experiences within each type of skill, for example, striking with different implements a variety of size and weight balls, coming at different heights and at different speeds. Schmidt proposes that all actions can be grouped into classes, for example, overarm throwing class, sideways striking class. These actions classes are represented in memory by generalized motor programmes (gmps). Each time a gmp is used, specific details such as the muscles, the force and speed are added to produce the desired action. Rather than every instance of each gmp being recorded in memory, only the relationships between the response details, the initial conditions existing when the skill is performed, the outcome and the sensory consequences are stored. These relationships form two rules or schema which enable the learner to produce relatively accurate novel versions of the action class, and to draw up accurate expectations of sensory feedback to be received from such novel movements. Schmidt's theory recommends that plenty of variety of movement experience should be encouraged so that the two rules which will be applied to each gmp will be well developed and hence more precise.

Movement education methods in gymnastics and dance, are clearly congruent with Schmidt's recommendations. Games teaching which is based on discovery learning and focuses on the development of a wide range of basic skills and concepts rather than restricting experience to traditional apparatus, techniques and rules is also highly desirable.

Cognitive Skills and Abilities

A deeper understanding of the cognitive involvement during the performance of motor skills has been made possible with the application of information processing models of behaviour.

Information processing is defined by Bruner (1972) as the way in which individuals achieve, retain and transform knowledge. The basic assumptions of information processing theory are that this processing can be broken down into sub-processes or components and that there are limits in the human capacity to process information. This limited capacity has been confirmed in studies of selective attention (Broadbent, 1958), memory span (Miller, 1956) and motor control (Kelso, Southard and Goodman, 1979).

The information processing model views the child as a complex machine which controls the flow of information from input to response. Information is sensed, briefly stored and that which is selected for further processing, perceived or interpreted. The processes of perception and response selection are heavily dependent on memory both of the immediate situation and of previous experience (see figure 7.2).

Although the model gives the appearance of sequential processing of information, more than one mechanism may be operating simultaneously. Figure 7.3 represents the processing involved in a skipping task. Parallel processing is evident for example in step three, when perception and response planning are both occurring, and in step 5 when perception and response implementation are operating.

An information processing framework is also useful for understanding how skills are learned. Gentile (1972) proposed that eight information processing steps constitute the first stage of initial skill acquisition and this is followed by the stage of skill refinement (see figure 7.4).

The first step is to understand the purpose of the task and the way the teacher introduces the task is critical. The goal should be clearly defined by the teacher or negotiated with the learner. It may be presented verbally or visually as a demonstration. Whether a precise recipe for success is given in terms of detailed guidance, or whether the child is encouraged to discover the optimum way of solving the problem will depend upon the task, the time which can be devoted to the learning process, the teacher's and the learner's preference. For example, in rock climbing, the child would hardly be encouraged to experiment with finding the best way of knotting a belay rope, and if the learner is lacking in confidence, past experience or cognitive skills a more highly guided approach may be advantageous. On the other hand, discovering the answer to a problem will involve more active cognitive involvement on the part of the learner, and more varied practice which Schmidt would see as beneficial to the development of schemata.

The important thing is that the learner understands what s/he is trying to achieve and the relevance of the task, but is not overloaded with things to remember.

The next two steps are to discover which stimuli or cues are relevant and then selectively attend to them. What should the learner look at, listen to, and when? Is it important to pay attention to how the movements feel? Which cues are unimportant and should be ignored? The teacher can facilitate selective attention by minimizing all but the relevant cues, gradually reintroducing them, or s/he can include them from the start, but direct the learner's attention to the relevant cues. The advantage of the latter approach is that the learner must develop the ability to resist distraction. However if the learner is by nature highly

Figure 7.2: A simple information processing model applied to motor performance

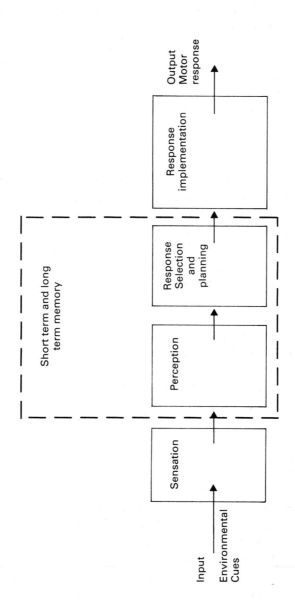

Figure 7.3: Cognitive involvement in a skipping task

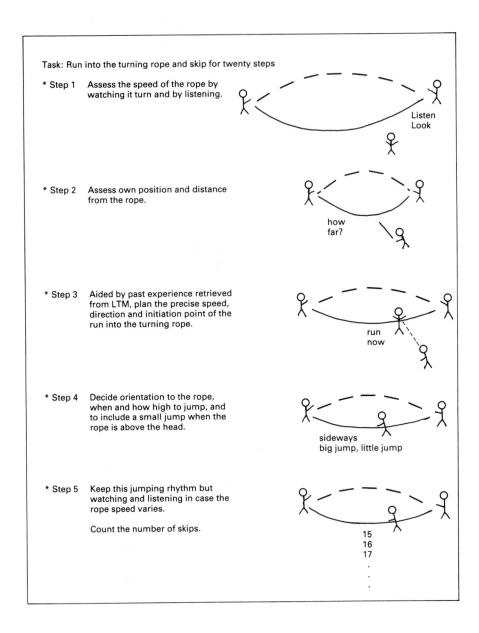

Task: Run into the turning rope and skip for twenty steps

* Step 1 Assess the speed of the rope by watching it turn and by listening.

Listen
Look

* Step 2 Assess own position and distance from the rope.

how far?

* Step 3 Aided by past experience retrieved from LTM, plan the precise speed, direction and initiation point of the run into the turning rope.

run now

* Step 4 Decide orientation to the rope, when and how high to jump, and to include a small jump when the rope is above the head.

sideways
big jump, little jump

* Step 5 Keep this jumping rhythm but watching and listening in case the rope speed varies.

Count the number of skips.

15
16
17
·
·
·

Figure 7.4: An information processing model of skill acquisition

	Initial Skill Acquisition							Skill Refinement
1	2	3	4	5	6	7	8	
Understand the purpose of the task	Discover which stimuli are relevant	Attend to relevant cues and ignore distracting cues	Plan response	Execute response	Examine feedback received during and after the response: did I succeed? did I do what I intended?	Plan next response in light of (6)	Execute response	Fixation: repeat correct response or Diversification: adapt response to meet varying situational needs

Source: Adapted from Gentile, 1972.

distractable, such an approach would only slow down the development of skill and possibly give rise to motivational problems.

The learner must now decide what response to make and plan it. The appropriate movements must be sequenced with the correct dynamics i.e., the overall speed of the action, the pattern of accelerations and decelerations within the action, the overall size and spatial orientation of the action, its overall and relative force. The amount and timing of guidance given by the teacher is important. If too many teaching points are given at once the learner will be overloaded. If s/he is allowed too much time to experiment s/he may find difficulty in modifying the developing action plan in the light of new advice. For example, Thomas, Pierce and Ridsdale (1977) investigating the effect of showing a model of efficient performance on a stabilometer balance task, at the beginning or midway through twelve practice trials, found that for both 7- and 9-year-olds, a model at the beginning facilitated performance, but if presented midway it had a detrimental effect on the younger children's performance.

The decision as to when to initiate the movement must be made and then the performance and its end result monitored.

The learner asks him/herself 'Did I succeed?', 'Did I do what I intended?'. Based on the answers, the learner can then plan his/her next response. If the outcome matched the goal the same action plan may be repeated. If the teacher sets a task which is easily accomplished unless new more demanding tasks follow fairly quickly, the learner may start to experiment with new personally modified goals. If this is actively encouraged by the teacher it will add to the learning experience of the child, but if the teacher is unaware that new goals are being tackled s/he may consider that the child is not trying, misbehaving or is incapable of the correct response.

If the response does not match the goal, the learner must evaluate if this was due to the inappropriateness of his/her performance or to some unpredicted factor in the environment. While the latter may well be the case, for example, when a shot at goal is deflected by another player, the former will occur frequently with learners.

There are several pieces of research which show that children do not always process knowledge of results effectively. For example, Barclay and Newell (1980) gave 8, 10 and 14-year-olds the chance to establish their own post knowledge of results (KR) time i.e., the time between the KR of one trial and the commencement of the next, in a motor memory task. The younger children always responded in less than five seconds suggesting that they were unaware of the value of KR in planning their next response.

However, Gallagher and Thomas (1980) showed that younger children (7-year-olds) performed less accurately than 11-year-olds on a motor memory task if their post KR processing time was restricted to three or six seconds. If this interval was raised to nine seconds both age groups performed equally well.

These two pieces of research suggest that the teacher must teach the learner to reflect carefully in his/her evaluation. S/he should encourage the learner to suggest what modifications should be made to his/her plan, only giving direct advice when the learner cannot produce an acceptable solution.

Once some degree of success has been achieved the learner passes into the skill refinement stage. Here, the learned response is either repeated during practice to develop consistency, or is adapted to meet varying situational demands. The former is appropriate for closed skills, i.e. skills which are performed in predictable, unchanging environments such as unopposed aiming skills like kicking at a stationary target, or many gymnastics and athletic skills. This type of practice would be totally inappropriate for open skills such as receiving and passing skills in team ball games which take place in constantly changing environments.

How quickly the teacher progresses from simple to more complex tasks must take into account each child's success, and this will probably mean groups of children tackling different tasks in the same class. It would be inconceivable for all children in a class to be on the same level reading task so why should all children to be given identical motor learning tasks?

It is obvious that the learner is faced with a vast amount of information to process and store. The capacity to process information is not unlimited but can a 10-year-old cope with more than a 6-year-old? Considerable research interest has been directed to the question of whether processing capacity changes with age, for example, Chi (1976), Connell (1984), Pascual-Leone (1970), and the consensus is that it is not actual capacity (structural capacity) which changes, but rather, the way in which the capacity is utilized (functional capacity).

Atkinson and Shiffrin (1968) used the term control processes to describe the ways in which the individual processes information.

Examples would be selective attention, labelling, organization and rehearsal.

There is research to show that in general, younger children exhibit less selective attention (Druker and Hagen, 1969) and less planful scanning (Vurpillot, 1968). Sugden (1981) using a modified video game called 'Variable Speed Brick Out', showed that younger children (7-year-olds) were less able than 12-year-olds to divide their attention 'efficiently'.

The game involved controlling a paddle on the screen in order to hit a moving ball and knock bricks out of a wall. At the same time, they were required to call out the score which appeared on the screen intermittently. Superior performance on both tasks showed the older children's capacity to handle greater processing loads.

Young children are also characterized by less spontaneous use of elaboration and information transformation strategies (Paris, 1978) and less rehearsal (Flavell, Beach and Chinsky, 1966). Sugden (1978 and 1980) examined the development of rehearsal in the visual motor and motor memory of 6 to 12-year-olds. The task involved moving a lever a criterion distance and then reproducing the same movement either ten or thirty seconds after. During the interval the boys either rested or counted backwards in threes. The latter condition prevented any rehearsal of the to-be-remembered movement. The results showed that 9 and 12-year-olds performed significantly worse when rehearsal was prevented while the 6-year-olds performed similarly in both conditions, suggesting that the younger children did not make use of rehearsal strategies.

Experimental evidence from Belmont and Butterfield (1971) and Debus (1970) shows that children can be taught to use strategies. If the same strategy is then to be used in other situations, the child must realize its value and its generalizability. A child may enter a new learning situation having recently been encouraged to use a labelling strategy, for example, labelling the hand entry position into the water in backstroke as 'five to one o'clock' or describing the early phase of the badminton overhead action as 'scratching the back'. The spontaneous use of this strategy in the new learning situation must not be taken for granted. The child may not see the generalizability of the strategy and will need prompting to use it.

The knowledge the individual has of his/her own capacities and the strategies s/he can utilize is known as metacognition. Brown (1974) describes it as the intention to be strategic. Kreutzer, Leonard and Flavell (1975) have reported that knowledge of memory capacity (meta-memory) increases rapidly around the age of nine, and that with this knowledge the use of chunking (grouping) and rehearsal strategies is readily seen. Lunzer (1968) has described the development of meta-cognition as a progression from 'doing a thing' to 'knowing what it is that one is doing'.

Campione, Brown and Ferrara (1982) consider that strategies are only beneficial to the extent that learners can anticipate their need, select from among them, oversee their operation and understand their significance. Being prepared to reject an unsuccessful strategy and try a new one is also important and seems to be an ability which develops over age. Paris and Cross (1983) wrote:

> The trademark of poor learning is not so much bewilderment about what to do as it is pursuit of inappropriate goals and the persistent application of inefficient strategies. The incorrigibility of young learners is due partly to the tenacity with which they cling to their beliefs about how to engage tasks.

An awareness of the child's knowledge about him/herself as a learner can only be gained through questioning, and careful observation of the way s/he tackles learning situations. The teacher should prompt children in the use of appropriate strategies. While s/he can provide these, for example, using the rhyme 'chin, knee, toe. Make a bow. See it go', to help the child remember the essential points of the shot put technique, a rhyme, label or image created by the learner him/herself will be even more effective.

If the teacher takes such an approach, s/he will not only be helping the child to acquire specific motor skills but also develop the child's learning skills and thereby his/her general intelligence. Garner (1978) described the hallmarks of intelligence as:

(a) generative, inventive and experimental use of knowledge rather than pre-programmed activities and;
(b) the ability to reflect upon one's own activity.

Affective Characteristics

If the learner is considered to be the single most important factor in the learning process, his/her feelings about him/herself, the task, the teacher and significant others are critical. Wheeler (1958) cited by Badger (1975) wrote,

> . . . the method an individual adopts in solving a problem is dependent as much on temperament as the development of reasoning ability. Emotional attitude is as important as cognitive capacity.

Each child will approach the learning task with a particular disposition. This will be made up of general enduring personality traits such as self-confidence, anxiety and persistence, and certain emotional states determined by the specific situation s/he finds him/herself in. For example, while the child may generally be a confident individual, a particular task, teacher, or context may cause feelings of low self-efficacy and subsequent low levels of motivation.

The point was made in the section on cognitive skills and abilities that the first task of the learner is to understand the goals of the task. If goals are to have incentive value and therefore merit investment of effort, they need to be specific, meaningful, challenging yet attainable. Easy goals have little incentive value and if accepted by the learner are pursued with little commitment. Goals which are too difficult reduce expectations of success and are poor motivators. Teachers must set attainable sub-goals if the ultimate goal is very difficult to achieve. Carron (1984) recommends that evaluation of progress towards goals should not be based on performance alone, but also on effort.

Evaluation of progress has typically been the province of the teacher, but it is important to recognize that the learner will also be making conscious or sub-conscious judgments about performance and progress, and the learner's judgment may not be congruent with that of the teacher.

A person's perception of the causes for an outcome influences subsequent motivation. If positive outcomes are perceived to be the result of internal personal factors like ability and effort, pride and satisfaction will be experienced and motivation levels will be high. If failure is attributed to the same internal factors, shame and dissatisfaction will probably result, and motivation levels will be low, with reduced persistence and involvement. Dweck and Goetz (1978) used the term 'learned helplessness' to describe this end result. The confidence with which a child approaches a task is influenced by previous successes and failures. Diener and Dweck (1978) have found that learned helpless-ness children underestimate the number of previous successes they have experienced and over-estimate the number of failures, and that even when they do succeed they attribute their success to external factors like luck or an easy task. Children need help in making accurate attributions for their performance. There is evidence from Diener and Dweck (1980) that retraining attributions can help learned helplessness children.

Roberts (1980) reported that below the age of 10 years children do not readily distinguish between effort and ability as the primary cause for good performance resulting in children of relatively low ability continuing to invest maximum effort. He found that only at 12 to 13 years of age did children become sensitive to the role their ability plays in outcomes. The age of involvement in serious sport is fast reducing and great care should be taken to avoid adults (teachers, coaches, parents) bombarding children with information on competence. The focus should continue to be on effort rather than ability.

It is also worth mentioning that boys and girls differ in their attributions. Females tend to evaluate their personal ability much lower before an event so they have a lower expectancy of success, while males more often enter achievement situations with a high expectancy of success. If they do succeed, males attribute their success to ability, whereas females refer to effort or more negatively to task ease or luck (McHugh, Duquin and Frieze, 1978). If males do fail, they preserve their self-concepts by typically attributing failure to bad luck or strong opposition. An awareness by the teacher of these differences should help in understanding learner's motivational states.

There is a widely held view that all young children enjoy games and physical activity. Research which has asked children to explain what they get out of sport and physical activity has found 'to have fun' to be frequently mentioned. In attempting to understand what is meant by fun, Passer (1981) considers that children probably experience 'fun' when their other primary needs are satisfied. These primary motives have been identified as affiliation, skill development, success and status, and excitement. The teacher must consider whether these motives can be satisfied in each lesson. If they are not, it is unlikely that learners will show high motivation levels.

The information value of feedback in skill learning has already been emphasized, but feedback has another dimension, that of social reinfor-cement. Improvements in self-esteem and in the quality of the teacher-learner relationship occur when children are given positive reinforcement. Carron (1984) has summarized research findings which reveal that younger children profit more than older ones, and that social reinforcement has its greatest effect when administered by a significant person of the opposite sex. It will only be effective if it is used selectively. Carron (*ibid*) writes,

> The teacher who says 'very good' after every performance by every student may create a positive, humanistic environment. However ultimately that encouragement will hold little incentive value and convey no information about performance effectiveness to the student.

The judicious use of positive social reinforcement is therefore critical if it is to have its fullest impact.

Conclusion

It should be evident that teachers cannot afford to neglect any single aspect of the learner, but must take into consideration the whole child: his/her physical, cognitive and affective characteristics. These are to a large extent dynamic variables being modified by every experience the child has. A sensitivity to the learner's aspirations, feelings and current physical and cognitive capabilities should produce well-motivated, successful learners who attribute their success to ability and effort.

Through skilful teaching which develops the skills of learning alongside the intended motor competencies, and encourages self-evaluation, the teacher and learner will be involved in physical education in its fullest sense.

References

ATKINSON, R.C. and SHIFFRIN, R.M. (1968) 'Human memory: A proposed system and its control processes', in SPENCE, K.W. and SPENCE, J.T. (Eds) *The Psychology of Learning and Motivation*, vol 2, New York, Academic Press.

BADGER, M.E. (1975) 'The influence of certain aspects of cognitive style on problem solving in 11–18-year-old boys and girls', MPhil dissertation, London, University of London Institute of Education.

BARCLAY, C.R. and NEWELL, K.M. (1980) 'Children's processing of information in motor skill acquisition', *Journal of Experimental Child Psychology*, 30, pp 98–108.

BELMONT, J.M. and BUTTERFIELD, E.C. (1971) 'Learning strategies as determinants of memory deficiencies', *Cognitive Psychology*, 2, pp 411–20.

BROADBENT, D.E. (1958) *Perception and Communication*, London, Pergamon Press.

BROWN, A.L. (1974) 'The role of strategic behaviour in retardate memory' in ELLIS, N.R. (Ed) *International Review of Research in Mental Retardation*, New York, Academic Press.

BRUNER, J.S. (1972) 'The nature and uses of immaturity', *American Psychologist*, 27, pp 687–716.

CAMPIONE, J.C., BROWN, A.L. and FERRARA, R.A. (1982) 'Mental retardation and intelligence' in STERNBERG, R.J. (Ed) *Handbook of Human Intelligence*, Cambridge, MA, Cambridge University Press.

CARRON, A.V. (1984) *Motivation: Implications for Coaching and Teaching*, Ontario, Sports Dynamics.

CHI, M.T.H. (1976) 'Short term memory limitations in children: Capacity or processing deficits?', *Memory and Cognition*, 4, pp 559–72.

CONNELL, R.A. (1984) 'Cognitive explanations of children's motor behaviour', unpublished doctoral dissertation, Leeds, University of Leeds.

DEBUS, R.L. (1970) 'Effects of brief observation of model behaviour on conceptual tempo of impulsive children', *Developmental Psychology*, 2, pp 22–32.

DIENER, C.I. and DWECK, C.S. (1978) 'An analysis of learned helplessness: Continuous changes in performance, strategy and achievement cognitions following failure', *Journal of Personality and Social Psychology*, 36, pp 451–62.

DRUKER, J.F. and HAGEN, J.W. (1969) 'Developmental trends in the processing of task-relevant and task-irrelevant information', *Child Development*, 40, pp 371–82.

DWECK, C.S. and GOETZ, T.E. (1978) 'Attributions and learned helplessness' in HARVEY, J., ICKES, W. and KIDD, R. (Eds) *New Directions in Attribution Research*, vol II, Hillsdale, NJ, Eribaum.

FITTS, P.M. and POSNER, M.I. (1967) *Human Performance*, Belmont, CA, Brooks/Cole.

FLAVELL, J.H., BEACH, D.R. and CHINSKY, J.M. (1966) 'Spontaneous verbal rehearsal in memory tasks as a function of age', *Child Development*, 37, pp 283–99.

GALLAGHER, J.D. and THOMAS, J.R. (1980) 'Effects of varying post KR intervals upon children's motor performance', *Journal of Motor Behaviour*, 12, pp 41–6.

GARNER, M. (1978) 'Commentary on annual awareness papers, *Behavioural and Brain Sciences*, 4, p 572.

GENTILE, A.M. (1972) 'A working model of skill acquisition with application to teaching', *Quest*, 17, pp 3–23.

KELSO, J.A.S., SOUTHARD, D.L. and GOODMAN, D. (1979) 'On the nature of human interlimb coordination', *Science*, 203, pp 1029–31.

KEOGH, J.F. and SUGDEN, D.A. (1985) *Movement Skill Development*, London, Collier Macmillan.

KREUTZER, M.A., LEONARD, C. and FLAVELL, J.H. (1975) 'An interview study of children's knowledge about memory', *Monographs of Society for Research in Child Development*, 40, p 159.

LUNZER, E.A. (1968) (Ed) *The regulation of Behaviour: Development in Learning*, 1, London, Staples.

McHUGH, M.C., DUQUIN, M.E. and FRIEZE, I.H. (1978) 'Beliefs about success and failure: Attribution and the female athlete', in OGLESBY, C.A. (Ed) *Women and Sport: From Myth to Reality*, Philadelphia, PA, Lea and Febiger.

MILLER, G.A. (1956) 'The magical number seven, plus or minus two: Some limits on our capacity for processing information', *Psychological Review*, 63, pp 81-97.

PARIS, S.G. (1978) 'Inference and transformation' in ORNSTEIN, P.A. (Ed) *Memory Development in Children*, Hillsdale, New Jersey, Eribaum.

PARIS, S.G. and CROSS, D.R. (1983) 'Ordinary learning: Pragmatic connections among children's beliefs, motives and actions' in BISANZ, J. and KAIL, R. (Eds) *Learning in Children: Progress in Cognitive Development Research*, New York, Springer-Verlag.

PASCUAL-LEONE, J. (1970) 'A mathematical model for the transition rule in Piaget's developmental stage', *Acta Psychologica*, 32, pp 301–45.

PASSER, M. (1981) 'Children in sport: Participation motives and psychological stress', *Quest*, 33, pp 231–44.

ROBERTS, G.C. (1980) 'Children in competition: A theoretical perspective and recommendation for practice', *Motor Skills: Theory into Practice*, 4, pp 37–50.

SCHMIDT, R.A. (1976) 'A schema theory of discrete motor learning', *Psychological Review*, 82, pp 225–60.

SUGDEN, D.A. (1978) 'Visual motor short term memory in educationally subnormal boys', *British Journal of Educational Psychology*, 48, pp 330–9.

SUGDEN, D.A. (1980) 'Developmental strategies in motor and visual motor short term memory', *Perceptual and Motor Skills*, 51, pp 146.

SUGDEN, D.A. (1981) 'Dual task performance: A developmental perspective', *Information Processing in Motor Skills, Proceedings of British Society of Sports Psychology*, pp 13–32.

THOMAS, J.R., PIERCE, C. and RIDSDALE, S. (1977) 'Age differences in children's ability to model motor behaviour', *Research Quarterly*, 48, pp 592–7.

VURPILLOT, E. (1968) 'The development of scanning strategies and their relation to visual differentiation', *Journal of Experimental Child Psychology*, 6, pp 632–50.

WADE, M.G. (1976) 'Developmental motor learning', in KEOGH, J. and HUTTON, R.S. (Eds) *Exercise and Sport Science Review*, Vol 4, California, Journal Publishing Affiliates.

Part C:
Issues Affecting Physical Education

Chapter 8:
Children with special needs

Lilian Groves

Physical education is more, not less, necessary for children with special educational needs than for their peers. Consider first those with obvious physical disabilities. They will have made and will continue to make visits to hospital so disrupting their schooling. Fear amongst parents and teachers of causing further physical injury may well mean that children are overprotected. They easily come to believe that they are incapable of physical activity. Their peers tend to share this view so that they are left out of informal play activities. This sedentary lifestyle can lead to obesity, circulatory and respiratory problems. Children have a poor self-image and tend to lack confidence both physically and socially. The need for a wide-ranging programme of physical activities with a good health-related fitness component is obvious. Consider next those whose physical problems are less obvious. Some children with moderate learning difficulties are as physically able as their peers but many suffer from difficulties in fine motor skills; often reaction times are slow; they fail to grasp the point of a game and are not wanted by their peers for informal play at break and after school. Failure in academic work combined with rejection at play may well exacerbate a sense of worthlessness. Some of these children are undersized and physically frail whilst others, like their physically disabled peers, often become obese. This group too, needs a well thought out physical education programme.

Already it would appear that we have begun to categorize children. The Warnock Report and the 1981 Education Act moved away from the old concept of labelling or categorizing children, towards a concept of what children need if they are to benefit from education (hence the term SEN, special educational needs). For administrative purposes it is often necessary to speak of children as having, say, visual impairment, but it is important to keep in mind that children grouped in this way do not form a homogeneous group. There is a huge gap between the performance and the problems of those with mild, and those with severe forms of the same disability. Even given the same degree of disability the personality of a child, together with the attitude of parents, siblings and doctors will influence the extent to which the disability becomes a handicap to living.

The 1981 Education Act was officially implemented by April 1983 but response to the Act differs greatly from one local education authority (LEA) to another. There is a popular belief that the desirability of integrating children with SEN into mainstream education was first articulated in the UK in this Act and the earlier Warnock Report. In fact section 33(2) of the 1944 Education Act provided that the great majority of all handicapped children should be educated in ordinary schools.

Chuter Ede said, 'Whilst we desire to see adequate provision of special schools we also desire to see as many children as possible retained in the normal stream of school life' (*Hansards* March 1944). The 1976 Act (section 10) also spoke of the intention to educate children with special needs in ordinary schools. However, section 10 was never implemented. Although there have always been some children with disabilities in ordinary schools, especially in infant schools, the majority received segregated education. During the 1970s and especially following the passing in the USA of Public Law 94-142 (Education of Handicapped Children) in 1975, parents and special interest groups in this country demanded an emphasis on 'normalization' for those with disabilities. From these protests came the Warnock Report and the less far-reaching 1981 Act. LEAs, sometimes for political, sometimes for economic, and sometimes for educational, reasons responded in a variety of ways.

In general there has been a growing emphasis on educating children in what has come to be known as 'least restrictive environment'. Some LEAs offer segregated education only to the most seriously disabled, while others maintain special schools for a much wider spectrum of disabilities. The majority have established special units attached to selected primary and secondary schools, while others permit enrolment (subject to the headteacher's agreement) in a neighbourhood school.

Even when children attend a mainstream school they are not

necessarily integrated for all or even a substantial part of the curriculum. The 1981 Act stated that where a child attends an ordinary school the LEA has a duty 'so far as is reasonably practicable' to provide opportunity for children to engage in the activities of the school together with children who do not have special needs. On the other hand it adds 'this is subject to the proviso that such involvement is not incompatible with the provision of efficient education for the children with whom he is educated' (section 2(31)). This proviso and the words 'so far as is practicable' make it relatively easy to 'excuse' children if there appears to be a problem — perhaps particularly in physical education.

However, it is assumed that the reader of this book will wish to provide physical education in the least restrictive environment and the rest of this chapter indicates how this may be achieved.

The 1981 Act defines a child with SEN as one who has 'learning difficulties which call for special education provisions to be made for him'. It enlarges upon this statement by explaining that a child is defined as having a learning difficulty if,

(a)   s/he has a significantly greater difficulty in learning than the majority of children of his/her age and,

(b)   s/he has a disability which either prevents or hinders him/her from making use of educational facilities of a kind generally provided in schools within the LEA concerned, for children of his/her age (section 1(4)).

The Physical Education Association (PEA) has elaborated on this definition within the context of physical education.

In response to questioning from a House of Commons Select Committee on SEN the PEA stated that

special educational needs might be brought about by a single factor or by a combination of factors including difficulties of body management, lack of manual dexterity, sensory impairment, obesity and emotional problems arising from any of these, but also from an inability to cope with cooperation/competition and also from a range of learning difficulties.

The Fish Report (1985) suggested that special educational needs frequently arise from the curriculum, from choice of teaching material and methods, and from the social and emotional climate in which an individual is placed. This points to an urgent need to examine both content and methods. Those who read this book will have already embarked upon this process.

Much evidence suggests that the attitude of the class teacher is the most important factor in the success or failure of mainstreaming. There is no doubt that providing for children with SEN puts considerable extra pressure upon teachers. Perhaps it is worth stressing that it is NOT unprofessional to be nervous or to feel inadequate when faced with children whose problems appear great; it IS unprofessional to take the easy way out and either 'excuse' children from physical education or subject them to situations in which we know they will fail. Teachers will need to be clear about their aims for those children without SEN and then to be prepared to modify objectives, material, organization and teaching style for children with SEN.

Preparations for Mainstreaming

Every child with a physical, sensory or learning disability will have been assessed before being placed in school. In the USA such an assessment would always involve a movement specialist; unfortunately this is not so in the UK. Some teachers are prepared to welcome a child with special needs into the classroom but feel that physical education is too much of a challenge. In the USA integration is often first practised in physical education, music and art and, such is the importance given to physical education, that it alone of all aspects of the curriculum is required by law for all 'exceptional' children.

Teachers in this country who believe in the value of movement education may have to initiate dialogue with parents, special needs advisers, physical education advisers and specialist agencies.

It is normal practice for a school in conjunction with the LEA to prepare for the reception of one or more children with disabilities by examining the environment for ease of access and so on. This may be the moment to consider the provision of specialized equipment for physical education or the need to adapt what is already available. Some authorities, for example, Kent, operate an equipment pool from which appropriate materials may be borrowed. Some of this equipment is commercially available, but some has been made in CDT (craft, design, technology) departments in secondary schools and polytechnics. It is well worth primary schools making contact with CDT departments to enlist their help. Those taking CDT at GCSE or 'A' level welcome a real design challenge.

Schools hopefully prepare staff and pupils as carefully as the environment. In some areas staff 'sensitizing' sessions are carried out. Those called to teach children who are hearing impaired can learn much from exposure to a video called 'Hearing through cracked glass' or similar material from the British Deaf Association. Similarly the Royal National Institute for the Blind can help those who will work with children with visual impairment to be more aware of specific problems. These are but two examples of ways of trying to understand children's difficulties. Experts from specialist organizations will willingly give advice (see lists at the end of the chapter).

Children, even quite young children, can learn to empathize through role play. What is it like to play games with a patch of gauze over one or both eyes? How do you turn over on the floor if you have no use of your legs? The point need not be laboured; teachers will find their own approach. Certainly, if possible, the incoming children should be invited previously to join the receiving class for a social occasion. Older individual children may be appointed as 'special friends' or 'buddies'. It is important that while children should be welcomed and supported, they should not be overwhelmed or overprotected by children, teachers or ancillaries.

It may be necessary to 'sell' physical education to parents and to children who may have led a very sedentary life. One way may be enlist the help of sportsmen/women, themselves disabled, who could show how sport and physical activity has enriched their lives. BSAD 1987 (British Sports Association for the Disabled), the Spastics Society and the Disabled Living Foundation would all give help over films to show parents, staff and older pupils, and the local branch of BSAD can advise on names and addresses of sportsmen and women who might visit the school. Many schools use the Olympics and other great sporting events as centres of interest; why not use the Paraplegic Games, the World Deaf Games and so on?

Contact with the school from which a child has come is obviously a necessity. Teachers should find out from their previous teachers just what a child CAN do. If children are mainstreamed from a special school then ongoing contact should be maintained. Special school teachers have much to offer those in mainstream education. Even if children come from another mainstream school, it is worth building bridges with the nearest special schools. Both schools can make use of the other's expertise and/or facilities.

Least Restrictive Environment or the Circular Ramp

The Warnock Report suggested ten variations of the level of provision based upon the notion of providing the least restrictive environment. The following is a model devised to show possible levels of provision in the context of physical education. There is nothing static about the proposals and a child may be at a different place in the ramp at different times.

Level One: Children are integrated for all aspects of physical education. In some cases this may be achieved without any special provision other than that the appropriateness of the curriculum for the whole group including those with disabilities, will have been established. In some cases integration will be achieved by the provision of special or adapted equipment. It may simply require the provision of larger or lighter bats and balls, larger targets or balls with a good texture for gripping. On the other hand, children may need wheeled support or trollies to join in with their peers (see Kent County Council, 1986). Further suggestions will appear under specific disabilities.

Level Two: Children are integrated for all aspects of physical education but also receive 'remedial' lessons. One LEA has devised a scheme involving parents taking small groups for an extra half hour a week. The parents receive careful guidance. More effective, probably, is a scheme whereby ancillary helpers and local sixth-formers take skill sessions planned by the class teacher or PE adviser for ten to fifteen minutes a day with those children who need extra input. Another project involves children who receive much of their education in special units but join their peers (in twos or threes) for physical education lessons. The class teacher ensures that the teacher(s) in charge of the unit(s) knows what is to happen in the physical education lessons so that they can prepare children beforehand.

Level Three: Is a combination of 2 and 3. Very often the class teachers would feel more able to integrate children if they had extra helpers in the physical education lesson. They should make full use of ancillaries, parents and community volunteers. Older children may act as 'buddies' working alongside a child in need of help. Obviously helpers must be advised on what is required and prevented from hindering children's growing independence. The teacher must at all time be in charge of the whole group.

Level Four: Children are integrated for some aspects of physical education but have special provision or join another class for other parts of the curriculum. For example, dance is the great 'integrator'. Gina Levete wrote a book entitled *No Handicap to Dance*. I used to say 'if you walk you can dance'. I now say 'if you can move your fingers you can dance'. In some cases outdoor games may pose a problem and in this case a child might join another class indoors for some other movement experience. The most common example is offering swimming with another class when peers are playing outdoor games, but dance could also be offered.

In some situations a wheelchair may present a hazard to able bodied children while other situations may present an unacceptable hazard for the child with the disability. While I have already emphasized the need to rethink the physical education curriculum to make for the most satisfying experiences for all, there may be some physical activities which teachers rightly feel should be offered to the majority but which may be inappropriate for a minority. As long as a real alternative is provided this seems to be entirely reasonable.

Level Five: Here the emphasis is on links with special schools to which children may go for PART of the PE programme. Obviously this is only feasible when a special school shares the site with a primary school.

Level Six: This entails totally segregated provision either in the ordinary school or the special school.

While these two levels may be regarded by some as a last resort and perhaps an admission of failure, they may actually be necessary as the first step along the ramp.

At least one LEA employs a specialist teacher who visits primary schools taking groups of children for segregated PE lessons. The real value of such a scheme might be realized by releasing class teachers to watch the work of the specialist as part of their in-service training.

Implementation of the Model

Teachers need a clear idea of the aims of physical education which are the same for all children. They need to be aware of the ability and the needs of individual children and to be able to fit the curriculum to the children rather than try to fit the children into an inflexible curriculum.

Undoubtedly it is to live in cloud cuckoo land to suppose that most teachers are able to produce a curriculum tailored to the needs of each individual. However, it is not unrealistic to hope that teachers will be able to identify what it is that they hope children will learn and to structure their teaching to that end. Furthermore, it is not inappropriate even at the primary level to think that children may become partners in their own education, that they may know what is expected of them and equally important, the purpose of what they are asked to do.

The class teacher must check with the headteacher that the child's doctor has given permission for the physical activities to which the child will be exposed. Clearly no-one wants to endanger a child, but the aim must be to allow all children to lead as normal a life as possible. Some children will be receiving physiotherapy and there should be careful liaison between school and therapist. Often the physiotherapist will advise not only on the appropriateness of an activity but the best timing for physical education in the child's day.

Warming up is an essential part of physical education. Asthmatics and those with physical disabilities in particular require a slow, extended period of limbering up. Naturally a teacher will plan a lesson with plenty of variety of pace, will evaluate progression and regularly review placement on the circular ramp.

Some Common Disabilities

It is inappropriate in a book of this nature to detail at length the medical, educational and social issues related to all the disabilities to be found in mainstream education. Interested teachers should turn to texts such as Gillham (1986). The outline below is given with particular reference to primary physical education.

Asthma

This is probably the commonest condition found in mainstream schools. Asthma comes from the Greek word 'to pant' and sufferers experience wheezing, breathlessness, coughing and tightness of the chest. Typically children miss a lot of schooling especially in winter and there is a tendency for them to be excused physical education. Yet with understanding and a proper use of drugs, asthmatics can lead normal lives.

There are many examples of first class sportsmen who suffer from asthma and who may provide role models or at the very least give doubting parents cause to rethink their attitude. Sportsmen include Alan Pascoe (Olympic silver medalist at hurdling) Chris Dury (Olympic gold medalist at rowing) and Ian Botham (cricketer extraordinary).

Asthma attacks may be brought on by a range of allergies, by cold and even by exercise. It is often psychosomatic, brought about by emotional upsets. Children can be taught to cope with attacks. Many carry inhalers which quickly correct the breathing pattern. Given training, and in particular, given a sensible attitude from parents and teachers, most asthmatics can cope with all aspects of physical education. Some children need to take medication before the physical education lesson and in all cases should be allowed to rest if an attack occurs during the lesson. The need for sensible warming up and for good changes of pace during the lesson have already been mentioned. Asthmatics who have been overprotected in their early years may suffer from poor posture and lack movement experiences. These can easily be dealt with in a well structured programme. For further details, contact the Asthma Society and read excellent articles in Groves (1985).

Epilepsy

This is another relatively common occurrence. According to a recent report, epilepsy is second only to migraine as Britain's commonest neurological problem. Thirty-six thousand new cases of epilepsy are diagnosed each year in the UK and one-third of these are children. There is a huge variation in severity of condition. Some children may have only one fit, and, because the condition is controlled with drugs, many never suffer another one. Others may suffer a fit twice a day.

There are many types of fit ranging from total loss of consciousness with convulsions, to 'absence' (previously known as 'petit mal'). The British Epilepsy Association has many useful publications including one written especially for school teachers. In simple terms a seizure is 'a burst of abnormal electrical activity in the brain' (Gillham, 1986). It is not a mental illness nor a sign of mental handicap nor is it an infectious disease, although the seizure can be very disturbing for the onlooker. 'Absence' on the other hand may pass quite unnoticed; the child looks blank, stares and after a few seconds returns to normal activity.

This may happen ten or twenty times a morning. A teacher may even unknowingly accuse a child of day-dreaming. It appears that 'absences' are more common if work lacks variety.

Major attacks (previously called 'grand mal' but now known as 'Tonic Clonic') require more attention. Movements should not be restrained nor, if possible, should the child be moved, but anything which may harm should be moved away. The head should be turned to one side and protected with a jumper or cushion. Once the convulsion is over, the teacher should talk reassuringly to the child. It is important that a teacher resumes the lesson as soon as the fit is over (or when someone can take over care) in order to reduce the dramatic effect for the rest of the class. Once children understand what is happening and see that their teacher is carrying on as normal, they tend to be quite matter of fact about the situation.

A third type of epileptic fit which affects only one part of the brain may result in irrational behaviour or confusion. This type of fit often lasts longer than others but is often looked upon as a behaviour problem rather than as the result of epilepsy.

Teachers must find out as much as they can about individual children. Doctors will advise on any necessary precautions but emphasis is upon normality.

A few general points may be made for physical education lessons. It may be necessary to forbid a child to go high on climbing apparatus and low level apparatus should always be provided offering similar tasks.

Mats should be placed around apparatus. Swimming presents some difficulties but the British Epileptic Association emphasizes the importance of learning to swim. The use of the 'buddy' system i.e. children working in pairs is a useful device. The child with epilepsy should be paired with a strong swimmer. The 'buddy' system is widely practiced in the USA for swimming lessons and partners' responsibility for one another's safety is reinforced by the whistle being blown from time to time during the lesson when partners must be able to touch one another. There should (as in any swimming lesson) always be a competent lifesaver on the bathside who will be able to hold a child's head above water if a fit takes place. There is a useful leaflet by the National Coordinating Committee on Swimming for the Disabled which notes that very few attacks actually occur in the water. Indeed as Robert Price (1980) points out '. . . epileptic attacks usually occur before or after activity but rarely whilst a child is actually performing'.

Incidentally Tony Greig is an epileptic — it did not prevent him from playing cricket for his country.

Diabetes

Harry Secombe, perhaps not renowned for his sporting prowess but certainly very active, is a diabetic and often speaks on behalf of the thousands of men, women and children in this country who are diagnosed as suffering from the disease. Although it is possible for children to have non-insulin-dependent diabetes the vast majority are insulin-dependent. Together with diet, twice daily injections of insulin are usually sufficient to keep diabetes under control in children. Quite young children learn to inject themselves. Exercise is an essential part of treatment and, unless specifically forbidden by a doctor, children can take part in all aspects of physical education. Nevertheless some precautions are necessary. Children will be advised by their doctor about having a snack mid-morning and mid-afternoon. If this is not normal practice in school those with this requirement should be permitted to have their snack with the least possible fuss and attention. The aim is to treat this group of children as normally as possible.

Precautions in physical education relate mainly to timing of activity. Many doctors advise that physical education should not take place immediately before lunch where blood sugar is low — the best time is usually half an hour after a meal. Check with the individual's doctor. Before strenuous activity it is advised that extra carbohydrate, for example, dextol or a bite size Mars bar should be taken. The correct footwear is also necessary and usually barefoot work is undesirable.

While emphasis is on 'normalization' the child should be watched carefully for any sign of reaction and if s/he complains of feeling dizzy, breathless or having pains s/he should stop exercise and receive care.

Heart Defects

It is normal practice whenever possible to place children with heart defects in ordinary schools. In some cases, but not all, the defect will be associated with other disabilities. It is essential to have written medical confirmation as to which activities are permissable. With heart conditions, even more than with others, it is impossible to generalize and each individual will be treated differently. Most children will want to be active and some, particularly at junior school age, do not know when to stop.

The teacher will be alert for signs of discomfort. Children should not be allowed to feel cold as this may bring on an attack.

All the above conditions might be regarded as 'hidden disabilities' and will have been recorded in ordinary schools for very many years. Our record of involving them in physical education and outdoor pursuit has not been good. Now that greater attention is focused on disabilities, the outlook for them is better. Every child wants to be thought normal and to participate with their friends.

Sensory Impairments

Hearing Impairment

Children who are hearing impaired can be fully integrated into physical education. The main problem is communication which is particularly difficult in a school hall or gymnasium where noise and vibration add to the distortion of sound. There are a few profoundly deaf children in normal classes but the majority will have some hearing. These children will wear hearing aids but in the gym these may be of limited use. Even skilled lip readers have problems in the hall and in outside games lessons.

Obviously the teacher must position himself and the child to the best advantage; a teacher must speak slowly and clearly. It is important to remember that speech development even amongst highly intelligent children is likely to be very slow. Instructions should be short and to the point and involve the use of body language. Demonstrations are important and sometimes manipulation is necessary. There will almost certainly be more direct teaching than normal. It is a good idea, if possible, to get a colleague or perhaps the teacher in charge of the 'deaf' unit to observe a physical education lesson and check on all those 'throw away' remarks which often accompany good teaching but are completely missed by a child with hearing problems. Communication may be less of a problem if the hall has a ring circuit and the teacher wears a microphone.

Sometimes however hearing aids need to be removed. Swimming is an obvious example and the use of the 'buddy' system (as outlined under epilepsy) is needed to ensure both easy communication and for safety purposes. Advice must be sought about the use of hearing aids in other circumstances.

All children enjoy rhythm and deaf children are no exception. In dance lessons rhythm may be beaten on the floor with a pole or the child may 'feel' the music through holding a balloon which will pick up vibrations. He may feel rhythm on percussion instruments. One of the finest young percussionists of today is profoundly deaf and there are professional dance groups made up of both hearing and deaf dancers. These provide good role models.

The use of scarves and large pieces of soft material helps children to move creatively and the teacher's own body language will enhance communication. The value of dance as a non-verbal means of communication is obvious. Less obvious, perhaps, is the value of dance in helping develop language. Wisher (1974) suggests that deaf children can learn many new words through movements expressing poems, songs and stories. They also learn 'movement' words and rarely forget words learned through a kinaesthetic experience.

Visual Impairment

Again emphasis is on finding out the nature of the impairment and any precautions necessary to prevent damage to residual sight. As in all other groups, children with visual impairment have many different problems. Some may be unable to distinguish between an object and the background. Attention to the colour of balls (yellow or bi-coloured), of posts (perhaps making them striped) and so on may be all that is necessary. Other children suffer from severely distorted vision, from lack of distance vision or from severe tunnel vision. Obviously tunnel vision makes for problems in team games, distance vision for skills such as striking or catching and so on. More worrying is a child with a detached retina. Here there will be clear limitations on what a child may or may not do.

All those concerned in the education of children with visual handicaps agree in the immense importance of developing independence. Mobility training involves body awareness, posture, locomotion, orientation and navigation skills, all of which clearly have a place in physical education. Formal mobility training is given by the 'mobility officer' but specialists like the schools to provide a range of physical skills. Hodgson (1985) emphasizes, 'All visually impaired pupils should take part in physical education lessons as they generally have little opportunity or motivation to bend, stretch, run, tumble and skip . . .'. Dodds (in Gillham, 1986) says that motor skills are 'best achieved through playing games . . . climbing, balancing, bouncing, swinging and the like'. Visually impaired children are likely to have a very poor body image, to be less fit because less active than their peers and to lack confidence and coordination.

An intervention programme (level 6 on the circular ramp) has been found to be important before integration. Duncan (in Groves, 1985) describes such a programme with pre-school children in preparation for an ordinary reception class.

It is always important to store apparatus and equipment with care but doubly so when the class includes children with impaired vision. Consistency in storage and placement is important. Obviously a good teacher will change the arrangement of large apparatus every few lessons. A child with visual problems must be taken to the piece of apparatus to feel the height and the relationship of one piece of equipment to another. He needs to know where to take off and to land, and if necessary, to count the number of steps required.

Modification of equipment has already been mentioned. Texture is important and may be particularly helpful in gymnastics where varying surfaces can help children to feel their way. Audio balls varying from ball bearings in a football to more sophisticated electronic devices can be bought or developed by electronics departments.

Children must have medical clearance for swimming since chlorinated water may be detrimental to the eyes. Usually children can wear goggles to cover contact lenses or other aids. It is helpful to have the swimmer in an easily identifiable cap and again the buddy system is useful. Obviously orientation may be difficult; ropes can be helpful and helpers on the side to prevent heads being bumped. Diving may be undesirable but again a doctor will advise directly or through the child's parents.

Because of lack of experience, the children may lag several years behind their contemporaries in movement skills. They are likely to need emphasis on health-related fitness as they go through the primary school. However, many will astound their teachers with their courage and eagerness to learn.

Physical Disabilities

Many children suffer not only from obvious physical disabilities, but from associated problems such as perceptual problems, sensory impairment and learning difficulties. Many will have missed a lot of school and it will continue to be disrupted with consequent social and emotional upsets. Some of those in mainstream schools will be in wheelchairs; more frequently they will be ambulant with or without aids.

A series of general questions might by put:

1   What can the child do? If he or she is transferring from a special school s/he may well have followed a quite demanding physical programme. To quote a much overworked, but nevertheless true saying, we must build on ability NOT disability.

2   Are there any activities forbidden on medical advice?

3   Is the child incontinent? If so how is this controlled? If by an appliance, where is this worn?

4   If the child wears calipers or prothesis may these be removed for physical education?

5   Does the child have hidden handicaps — perceptual motor problems, visual defects, a heart defect . . .?

6   Does the child feel the cold quickly?

7   Is the child on regular medication? Are there any side effects?
8   What advice on posture is offered by the physiotherapist?

These questions should be answered before the child is admitted to mainstream education.

The ancillary supplied by the LEA should be trained to play an effective part in increasing the child's independence and self image. The physical education programme should only be drawn up after a full discussion with all interested parties.

Only a brief account of the main forms of disability found in mainstream schools if given here. More detail is given in such publications as Gillham (1986).

Cerebral Palsy

This title covers a range of disabilities all of which are forms of motor disorders due to non-progressive brain damage.

Over 60 per cent of sufferers are spastic, that is, they have increased muscle tone and excessive stretch reflexes. Muscles contract strongly leading to abnormal postures. The term hemiplegia is used to indicate paralysis of one side of the body while monoplegia is paralysis of one limb and quadriplegia is paralysis of all four limbs.

Athetoids demonstrate involuntary uncoordinated purposeless movements.

Ataxics suffer from dizziness and disturbed balance with lack of muscle coordination.

Those children with more severe forms of cerebral palsy will probably be in special schools. However to judge by letters reaching the Spastic Society each week, teachers in mainstream schools are working with increasing numbers of children with cerebral palsy.

A few of those will be able to walk with or without assistance and may be able to join in all activities, while others need to achieve a stable base to perform any movement skill. The physiotherapist will advise on the most appropriate position for each individual. Care must be taken to avoid injury due to insensitivity in the limbs.

It should be remembered that fast movements may both encourage the use of bad movement patterns and induce spasm, as may loud noises. Children can be helped to control their response to noise over a period of time.

Children in wheelchairs which they control can often take part in a wide range of activities. The danger may be to other children and it may be necessary to allocate separate space. Wheelchairs slalom courses may be set up on a permanent basis to encourage skilful handling.

Children can leave their wheelchairs to take part in gymnastics but advice from physiotherapists must be followed with regard to positioning. Swimming is perfectly possible but it is important to watch carefully in case a child goes into spasm in the water.

Few quadriplegics in electric wheelchairs will be found in mainstream schools and where they are, level 5 or 6 in the circular ramp may need to be employed.

Many remarks made about spina bifida will apply to cerebral palsy.

Spina Bifida

There are increasing numbers of children with this condition in ordinary primary schools. The condition is caused by a failure in spinal development before birth so that the spinal cord is exposed and damaged. This condition leads to varying degrees of paralysis of the lower limbs and trunk, and frequent inability to control the muscle of the bowel and bladder. Hydrocephalus (a build-up of fluid in the brain) commonly accompanies spina bifida. The teacher should always know if a Spitz Holter or Pudenz valve or shunt has been fitted and should be aware of the signs of blockage of the valve. The early signs are likely to be drowsiness, headache, irritability and loss of concentration.

Children with a relatively minor degree of spina bifida are likely to be in a mainstream school and to move with calipers and sticks. Even with this group, lack of sensation in the lower limbs mean that a careless movement against a rough surface will damage the skin which may take weeks or even months to heal. Children need to be taught how to take care of their lower limbs. Children should wear tights and socks — even for swimming. Where a bag is worn this must be emptied before the lesson in the hall or swimming bath and care must be taken not to squash the bag or pull it out of position.

All this said, with appropriate assistance, children with spina bifida can take part in all those activities which do not rely on the use of the legs, for example, dance. In wheelchairs they can participate in many games activities, but it is likely that their ball skills will be less developed than those of their peers. This is due to a lack of movement experience both pre-school and in their earlier school years. They may well need special programmes to improve their skills (level 2 or even level 3 on the circular ramp as a first step).

Childhood Arthritis or Still's Disease

Joints become tender and swollen and extremely painful. While it is desirable to encourage movement in the joints, this should only be attempted under the guidance of the physiotherapist. However, swimming is highly recommended, since this is not weight-bearing. Often the children can join in aspects of dance and some small apparatus work but jumping should be avoided.

Moderate Learning Difficulties

Clearly children suffering from many of the disabilities described above will have learning difficulties either because of broken schooling, or because of associated conditions, for example, spatial problems amongst children with cerebral palsy. However, those included in this section are those whose learning problems arise from mental retardation or from social conditions. Research, (for example, that of Rarich and Dobbins, 1971 — see Groves, 1979) indicates that, while as a group children with learning difficulties are significantly poorer than their peers in a wide range of motor tasks, some are better than average. Experienced teachers will recognize that those who are physically able gain greatly if their skills are recognized and valued. It may be less obvious that self-esteem can be as low as physical ability! Children who lack physical skill need to experience success in an area of the curriculum which offers immediate feedback — good or bad. Incidentally it should be borne in mind that while many slow learners are physically clumsy, not all clumsy children are intellectually retarded (see below).

Where level 2 provision on the circular ramp can be made, that is, some extra 'remedial' lessons in small groups, children with learning difficulties will be happier and more successful in main class physical education than in academic subjects. Children need considerable individual attention.

Lessons should be structured so that there is good variety to prevent boredom yet not so many changes of focus as to cause confusion. The teacher must analyze tasks and set short term, easily obtainable goals (see Brown, 1987, for good task analyis). Children are freqently confused by what John Holt in *Born to Fail* described as 'the torrent of words pouring over them'. Instructions should be both clear and brief and should be accompanied by gesture and modulation of the voice to get the message across. It goes without saying that the teacher must have every child's attention before giving instructions and that children should be well spaced to avoid silliness. Feedback and encouragement are essential as are careful evaluation and provision of progressively more difficult tasks.

Individual activities, requiring the child to concentrate on one thing at a time, are obviously easier than say group games where the child has to respond not only to a moving object but also to other players and cope with the whole business of space awareness. This is not to say that, given basic skills, they cannot succeed in and enjoy small-scale games. Dance has proved to be particularly successful with both boys and girls. Research by Groves (1975) showed that following a term of extra classes in dance, slow learning girls, mainly from deprived homes and with considerable behaviour problems, greatly improved in concentration in a variety of situations. Displays of aggression and anti-social behaviour dropped significantly. Children who are withdrawn can be given material to focus upon or can wear masks which make them feel 'invisible' and therefore more courageous. By integrating dance with a thematic approach to learning, language, art, music and other aspects of the curriculum may well become more accessible to the child with moderate learning difficulties. Many of the suggestions in the next two sections apply also to this group.

Emotionally Disturbed Behaviour

We are not here thinking of naughty children but those who are receiving or need to receive psychological help. In many cases, the problem arises from one or more of the disabilities mentioned above. In other cases, it arises from an inability to make good relationships. Mention has already been made of dance as a means of reducing aggression. (It may be worth giving a word of warning over choice of music in dance; a wrong choice may create a highly undesirable response.) It is clear that highly competitive situations can produce outbreaks of temper as will tasks seen as too difficult by the child. Emphasis should be placed on cooperation not competition.

In dance there are many opportunities for partner work and for developing trust but also a teacher may set tasks which can only be achieved successfully by two (or more) children working together. Outbursts are often accompanied by either 'it's not fair' or 'I can't'. The latter can be avoided if the task is set at an appropriate level. Every attempt must be made, not only to BE fair but to be SEEN to be fair. A group of very disturbed children working on a task which was timed were satisfied by being able to watch a giant egg-timer (home-made from two plastic bottles). It was seen to be fair.

Children can be very disturbed by too much choice, so only a limited variety of equipment should be put out and sufficient of that to go round if a choice has to be made.

Clumsy Children

Research carried out in the seventies (see Groves, 1979) indicated that 5 per cent of the school population experience motor problems. In other words, every class of primary school children is likely to have at least one child who is physically awkward.

Some exhibit extreme awkwardness in gross motor tasks while others' problems may lie in the realm of fine motor tasks. As the children move up the primary school, the gap between their performance and that of their peers widens. These children have special educational needs as much as any of those described above. Henderson (1984) — see Groves (1985) stated that 'the notion that there is only one type of clumsy child who needs one form of treatment is a myth!'

It is important to recognize that the child continually knocking things over, falling down in the playground and so on really does need help. In extreme cases, clinical help is essential. Most large conurbations have a clinic for children who are motor retarded. For these and for less disabled children, PE lessons can be sheer misery. Much of what has been said above on breaking down tasks into easily achievable components, emphasizing cooperation rather than competition, and offering extra remedial lessons applies here.

A useful description of one remedial programme by Gallagher appears in Groves (1985) and in the same publication Cooke directs attention to research in this important area. Sugden and Waters (n.d.) provide an extensive bibliography.

Conclusion

The reader will have noticed avoidance of terms such as 'handicapped children', 'special needs children' even 'disabled children'. Those we teach are first and foremost children and disability and needs are secondary. This is not mere semantics. Children with SENs are more like their peers than unlike and should be treated as such. Many suggestions in this chapter — the need to plan progressive programmes based on evaluation of children's work, to have clear goals, to individualise the work and so on — apply equally to PE with all children.

There have always been children in schools for whom PE is something to be avoided. It is my firm belief that in providing appropriate experience in PE for those identified as having special educational needs, we will make a very positive contribution towards the further development of all children.

References

BROWN, A. (1986) *Active Games for Children with Movement Problems*, London, Harper and Row.

BROWN, A. (1987) 'The integration of children with movement problems into the mainstream games curriculum', *British Journal of Physical Education*, 18, 5, pp 230–2.

FITT, S. and RIORDAN, A. (Eds) (1980) *Dance for the Handicapped*, Washington, DC, American Alliance for Health, Physical Education, Recreation and Dance.

GILLHAM, B. (Ed) (1986) *Handicapping Conditions in Children*, London, Croom Helm Special Education Series.

GORDON, N. and McKINLAY, I. (Ed) (1980) *Helping Clumsy Children*, Edinburgh, Churchill Livingstone.

GROVES, L. (1975) 'Physical Education for Slow Learning Girls in North Eastern Schools', Unpublished MEd thesis, Durham University.

GROVES, L. (Ed) (1979) *Physical Education for Special Needs*, Cambridge, Cambridge University Press.

GROVES, L. (1982) 'The Warnock Report — A charter for all children', *Prince Philip Fellows' Lecture*, London, PEA.

GROVES, L. (Ed) (1985) *Who Cares? A Collection of Papers for Caring Physical Educationists*, London, PEA.

GROVES, L. and MIDGLEY, C. (Ed) (1986) *Physical Education and Recreation for People with Special Needs: An Annotated Bibliography*, London, PEA.

HARRISON, J. (Ed) (1986) *Swimming for those with Special Needs*, Loughborough, ASA.

HODGSON, A. (1985) 'How to integrate the visually impaired', *British Journal of Special Education*, 12, 1, pp 35–7.

JORDON, I. (1987) *'Physical education for slow learners'*, *British Journal of Physical Education*, 18, 5, p. 233.

KENT COUNTY COUNCIL EDUCATION DEPARTMENT (1986) *Physical Education for Pupils with Special Educational Needs in Mainstream Schools*, Maidstone, Kent County Council, Education Department.

LEVETE, G. (1982) *No Handicap to Dance*, London, Souvenir Press Ltd.

MILES, A. and KNIGHT, E. (1987) 'The contribution of PE to the general development of children with special educational needs', *British Journal of Physical Education*, 18, 5, pp 204–6.

PRICE, R.J. (1980) *Physical Education and the Physically Handicapped Child*, London, Lepus Books.

SUGDEN, D.A. and WATERS, C. (n.d.) *Children with Movement Problems (Annotated Bibliography)*, Leeds, School of Education, University of Leeds.

WISKER, P. (1974) 'Therapeutic values of dance education for the deaf', in *Focus on Dance*, VII, 3rd edn., AAHPER.

Some Relevant Organizations

Association for Children with Heart Disorders, 536 Colne Rd., Reedley, Burnley, Lancs.

Association for Spina Bifida and Hydrocephalus, Tavistock House North, Tavistock Sq., London, WC1 9HJ.

Asthma Society, 12 Pembroke Sq., London, W2.

British Epilepsy Association, Crowthorne House, New Wokingham Rd., Wokingham, Berks, RG11 3AY and 40 Hanover Square Leeds, LS3 1BE.

British Sports Association for the Disabled (1987), Hayward House, Barnard Cres., Aylesbury, Bucks, HP21 9PP.

National Deaf Children's Society, 31 Gloucester Place, London, W1.

National Diabetes Association, 177A Tennison Rd., London, SE25 5NF.

Physical Education Association of Great Britain and Northern Ireland (PEA), 162 King Cross Rd., London, WC1X 9DH.

Royal National Institute for the Blind, 224 Great Portland St., London, W1N 6AA.

Royal National Institute for the Deaf, 105 Gower St., London, WC1E 6AH.

Chapter 9:
Girls and Boys Come Out to Play
(But Mainly Boys) —
Gender and Physical Education

 Anne Williams

> I don't really mind that girls don't play. Who cares about girls?
> (7-year-old boy)

This chapter examines the implications for physical education of the adoption of a variety of different stances towards equality of opportunity. The first part discusses some of the issues which arise in moving towards a policy of equality of opportunity and considers the extent to which equality of opportunity in fact maximizes the chances of girls achieving their potential. The second section asks some practical questions.

Gender and Physical Education

Two issues concerning gender and physical education need to be discussed. The first is the extent to which physical education teaching reinforces stereotyped images of masculinity and femininity which may also be perpetuated through classroom practice in other subjects. The second is the question of the extent of the gender specificity of physical activities and how all pupils can best be encouraged to maximize the development of their physical abilities.

This section will look at some of the ways in which the educational system works to the disadvantage of one sex and will illustrate some aspects of this by reference to discussion held with junior school pupils. The comments made by pupils are from interviews held by the author with 7, 10 and 11-year-old junior school pupils. Seventy pupils were interviewed. Semi-structured discussions took place with groups of three pupils in which they were encouraged to express views or comment on various topics related to physical education and sport. The author was very conscious of the need to avoid leading pupils to make comments or give answers which they saw as desirable rather than those which reflected their own views. In the event the children were, almost without exception, more than willing to talk and little prompting was needed other than occasional interventions to introduce a new idea or to bring the discussion back to the point when it strayed too far from the issues at hand for too long. Nevertheless, it has to be recognized that the mere fact of being interviewed by a woman rather than by a man inevitably introduces the possibility of unmeasurable influences upon the pupils' perceptions of the matters under discussion.

The Sex Discrimination Act prompted the examination of all existing curricula since operating any quota system based on sex or the exclusion of either sex from any curriculum activity was now illegal. Primary school physical education has tended to be ignored by those looking at the gender issue in physical education, perhaps because the more obvious divisions which operate at secondary school level appear to be absent. However, the assumption that, by teaching physical education to mixed groups or by offering equivalent activities in games lessons, boys and girls receive equal opportunities reflects an approach to the issue which is limited in its conception and in its impact.

Even at this level, only the infant teacher could claim to be operating an equal opportunity policy in physical education, since at this age children are usually being taught in mixed sex groups for all of their physical education lessons. Junior school pupils are frequently segregated by sex for games lessons. Since, at this age, there are no significant physical differences between boys and girls, indeed girls are frequently bigger and stronger than their male contemporaries, there seems to be no sound physical basis for such practice. The games skills which form the basis for the adult game forms which will be introduced at a later stage are relevant to both boys and girls. Discussion with junior school pupils reveals an awareness that differences in performance result from factors other than innate physical differences. Comments tended to focus upon football and gymnastics, two activities which were familiar to both boys and girls, and which were seen as the province of one sex more than the other.

> Yes, they (the girls) can play it (football) — I mean if they started at the time we started they could be just as good.) (11-year-old boy)

> They say all the boys are better than the girls, but if the girls practised a lot they could be better. (11-year-old boy)

> They don't have much of a chance to do it (football) do they? (11-year-old boy)

> I've seen a game where the ladies played the men and the ladies won and beat the men. (11-year-old boy)

> Boys aren't as keen (on gym). Girls practise at home while boys like going out. (11-year-old girl)

> We don't put our effort into doing gym. (10-year-old boy)

> Some boys are better than girls (at gym) if they've been taught well. (10-year-old girl)

> I suppose it depends — if you want to be strong you can be strong, and if you don't, you don't. I don't want to be. (11-year-old girl)

It is important to recognize that, while there are no physical reasons for differences in performance among pre-pubertal boys and girls, social mores and pressures lead to different lifestyles which affect attainment. From an early age, differences in experience of physical activities and in activity interests tend to produce differences in performance or aptitudes of which the pupils are well aware.

> Girls are better at things like the splits and cartwheels. (11-year-old boy)

> Girls are more double jointed than boys. (11-year-old boy)

> Boys have got better skills (ball games) than girls. (10-year-old boy)

> Boys can't skip and they can't do much cartwheels and they can hardly do a gambol (forward roll). (7-year-old girl)

Factors such as playtime activity reinforce these differences.

We just walk around. They (the boys) take the whole field up playing football. (11-year-old girl)

They should cut the playground in half so the girls can have one half and the boys the other. (10-year-old girl)

Most of us play football. (11-year-old boy)

We just walk around with friends. We prefer it. (11-year-old girl)

Primary age children already have clear ideas of what constitute 'girls' and 'boys' activities.

Boys train for different things. They'd think, I'm not a girl, I'm not playing that game. (11-year-old girl)

Well the girls wouldn't want to play football as much as the boys would they? We don't want to play netball do we? (11-year-old boy)

I think girls are better at skipping and boys at football. (7-year-old boy)

The differential treatment of boys and girls from an early age in terms of approved play activities is well documented. Because boys tend to play football with their fathers and their friends and receive encouragement to do so they are likely to be more skilful and more knowledgeable about the game than their female peers. One solution could be some kind of compensatory teaching for girls or for single sex teaching of the same activity so that differences in ability and experience may be taken into account. However, whether divisions on grounds of gender are the best means of accounting for ability differences is highly questionable. In any primary school class, the differences within one gender group are likely to be at least as great as the differences between them. Ability grouping would almost certainly produce mixed sex groups although the distribution of the sexes in the different ability groups might be expected to vary. A teaching style which allows for differentiated tasks and variously modified games in order to cater for groups of differing ability or experience should enable all pupils to work to the best of their ability. The difficulty of implementing such a policy, particularly for the inexperienced teacher, should not, however, be underestimated.

Activities which are seen as gender-specific are, of course, not all male-focused, although 'male' activities are generally seen as more prestigious. Boys can be disadvantaged as well as girls. Dance is the clearest example of an activity seen as inappropriate for boys. Unfortunately, most junior schools are unable to provide dance as a part of the physical education curriculum (apart from movement lessons using radio programmes), thus both boys and girls are being denied the opportunity to achieve in this area of the physical education curriculum.

Gymnastics is also an activity which is perceived by pupils (and unfortunately also by some teachers) as an activity in which girls excel, as evidenced by the comments made by the pupils interviewed. It is also, of course, an activity which is presented by the media as a 'feminine' activity, one in which, at the highest levels, grace and aesthetic appeal are emphasized while the strength and other physical qualities required are underplayed. The fact that boys tend to regard gymnastics as a 'girls' activity and thus as cissy means that it is perceived as a part of the curriculum of less importance than higher prestige 'male' activities. Also, boys with particular talent in this area are less likely to gain recognition for it.

A first step in implementing a policy of equal opportunity would therefore be to remove the obvious discrimination which exists where a different and arguably inferior curriculum is offered to the girls. However, equality of access is only a first stage if indeed it is any answer at all. It is quite obvious that offering girls and women equal access to activities and facilities does not produce equal participation. This has been clearly demonstrated among the adult population.

The targetting of women by the Sports Council in their ten-year policy arises from a recognition that far more positive steps are needed than merely making facilities available at convenient times of the day. Similarly, simply making an identical curriculum available will not produce equal opportunities or remove gender stereotypes. The views of the 7-year-olds interviewed by the author are evidence of the formation of stereotyped images of appropriate boys and girls activities, in spite of having followed an ostensibly identical physical education curriculum.

In looking at what is offered to boys and girls under the physical education umbrella, it is important to consider the extra-curricular opportunities offered to pupils as well as the formal curriculum. Since physical education post-holders tend to be male, and since more male than female teachers are involved in extra-curricular physical education in the primary school (Williams, 1980), there are likely to be far more opportunities for boys to take part in extra-curricular physical activities than there are for girls. Simply opening such opportunities up to both sexes is unlikely to produce mixed sex groups, as evidenced by the reaction to just such an initiative (May and Ruddick, 1983). The school had been told that football training was to be made available to all boys and girls.

> There was immediate uproar from the boys. They did not want girls to join in and showed marked hostility and antagonism to the idea. The girls were immediately put off and there was some ill-will and tension between the girls and the boys during the next few days.

The image presented by schools in which the only involvement in extra-curricular activity is by men and where the majority if not all of the participants are boys, has to be that physical activity is a male rather than a female domain. This image will be conveyed to infants and juniors alike. Offering the same curriculum while extra-curricular opportunity heavily favours boys cannot provide equal opportunity at any level. This issue of access cannot, of course, be solved by the school alone. Media attention in relation to this issue has focused on examples of junior age girls wishing to play football in leagues under the jurisdiction of the ESFA which forbids mixed teams. The answer has been that offering an equivalent activity meets the letter if not the spirit of the law. This in itself is a rather dubious argument. More important is the fact that netball is not equivalent to football neither is rounders equivalent to cricket. As Talbot (1986) points out, the differences in prestige accorded to the male and female activities, in their adult game form mean that the girls are inevitably being offered an inferior curriculum diet and are receiving many hidden messages about the status of their games. They are being taught games which are seen as non-serious and which are rarely if ever pursued in adult life, in sharp contrast to the high profile professional team games being taught to the boys.

We shall return to the issue of curriculum content later, however it should be noted that many aspects of classroom practice, over and above the actual lesson content may affect the perceptions which girls and boys have of different curriculum activities. As Evans (1984) points out, there are a host of practices which may on the surface seem trivial, which contribute to the conceptions which pupils hold of masculinity and femininity. Moreover, many pupils arrive at school aged 5 already socialized into male and female roles within families where sexual division of labour is overt and sharply defined. If such a division of labour is also perpetuated in the school then the impact of an equal opportunity or anti-sexist philosophy will be limited. There are many instances which could be given as examples. Requests for help with apparatus in PE from 'a couple of strong boys' have little logic in a class of pre-puberty children where the strongest children in the class are quite likely to be female. Equally unsatisfactory in terms of the image of masculinity and femininity presented are organizational arrangements whereby some fourth year boys have the task of putting out the large apparatus in the hall on designated days each week.

Many other examples could be given of aspects of school life which reinforce the 'masculine' nature of participation in sports. Reading schemes provide one such example. Lobban (1987) divided sex roles found in reading schemes into those prescribed for girls only, for boys only and for both sexes. There are no instances of sports activities being ascribed either to both sexes or to girls only, the nearest being skipping which is prescribed for girls. Under boys' activities or skills, in contrast, are found playing football, playing cricket, sailing boats and playing sports. The presentation of positive images for both sexes should transcend subject boundaries.

Many instances may be cited where teachers who claim to treat boys and girls the same actually tolerate different standards from boys and girls and also categorize the same behaviour differently depending upon whether its perpetrator is male or female (Clarricoates, 1980). This happens in responses to behaviour related to curriculum tasks as well as in more general ways, and operates from the reception class onwards. Aggressive behaviour can be encouraged as appropriate in a boys game while the same behaviour from girls in a game results in rebukes for unladylike behaviour. A girl will be complimented for looking good when performing a particular gymnastics skill while a boy performing the same skill will be praised for his strength. The author remembers watching a student teacher exhorting the girls to 'make your sequence look pretty' then telling the boys whose demonstration followed to 'give it all you've got'! The original task set had been identical.

So far the discussion has focused upon the desirability of giving both sexes access to the same curriculum and of avoiding differential treatment of boys and girls on gender grounds. The problems faced by the teacher attempting to put such a philosophy into practice should not be underestimated. The fact that boys tend to receive more of the teacher's attention than girls is well documented. This is not always easy to overcome in the classroom where the penalty for ignoring boys who are socialized into expecting the lion's share of attention may well be considerable disruption. In the hall using large apparatus safety has to be taken into consideration. For the non-specialist teacher older junior pupils who enjoy the physical challenge of using higher equipment or trying to see whether they can get further or higher are often a threat. Again because of socialization, they are more likely to be boys than to be girls who, by the age of 11, have all too often learned that physical challenges are not perceived as appropriate feminine pastimes.

Equality of access is however only part of the problem. We have been talking about access to an essentially 'male' world. Weiner (1985) describes this as an 'equal opportunities' perspective, that is, providing equal access for both boys and girls to existing educational benefits. This perspective encourages girls to compete successfully for access to the advantages currently enjoyed disproportionately by boys. It can be seen in the Association of Women Tennis Professional's demands for equal television coverage and equal prize money to that enjoyed by the top male professionals.

It should be noted that, while boys are the main benefactors under the present system which accords more time and prestige to male sports, they can also be disadvantaged. This is particularly relevant at the primary stage where 'masculine' behaviour is often tolerated from girls, albeit on the basis that they will eventually 'grow out of it'. It is far more socially acceptable to be a girl who is a 'tomboy' than to be a boy who is a 'cissy'.

An 'anti-sexist' perspective, on the other hand, concentrates on the development of girl-centred education. Female culture has to be recognized as at least equal, if not superior, to male culture. This clearly has quite different implications for curriculum practice. Boys participate in many physical education activities which are directly related to adult sport forms which are significant activities in adult male culture. For girls, this relationship between adult culture and school physical education simply does not exist. For many girls, growing up means growing out of playing games, because they are not seen as having any significance in adult female life. There is then a discontinuity between being a girl and being a woman which does not apply to boys as they become men. Thus, as Talbot (1986) points out, while some boys games become or help boys to prepare for men's sports, the same is not generally true of girls' games.

It was interesting to note that when the boys and girls interviewed were asked what activity they would like to be really good at, few of the 7-year-old girls mentioned activities outside their school physical education experience in contrast to the boys who had already formulated clear ideas of activities which could be appropriate for them as adults such as skiing, golf and athletics. By the age of 11 the boys aspirations were far more clearly orientated towards 'male' adult sports, mainly football and basketball. The girls had by this age widened the range of activities mentioned but these were either much less gender specific, or, in the case of netball mentioned by several, were activities where opportunities for adult participation are severely limited compared with opportunities available to men to play team games. Boys had thus identified activities which were likely to be available to them as adults, in contrast to the girls, who were identifying activities which were unlikely to be real possibilities for them when they grew up.

Equal access to curriculum activities therefore does not necessarily lead to equal access to physical activity as a leisure pursuit. At secondary level this frequently poses serious difficulties in motivating adolescent girls. Until a relationship exists between girls' curriculum experience and outside or post-school opportunities which is comparable to that which exists at present for boys, this aspect of equality will not be achieved. While this is clearly a particular problem for those teaching in secondary schools, it should be remembered that primary school physical education not only provides an educational experience for children aged 5-11, but is also a foundation on which secondary school physical education builds. Because of this, factors which are relevant at secondary level should be considered by the primary school teacher.

There are thus various interpretations of equality of opportunity. Supporters of feminism, advocates of equality of opportunity and women's liberationists do not speak with one voice. The adoption of a radical feminist position involves the identification of men as the problem and demands the recognition of female culture as at least equal, if not superior, to male culture. This has quite different implications from the adoption of a socialist feminist position which encourages women to compete successfully for access to advantages currently

enjoyed disproportionately by men, such as equal pay, equal employment opportunities through provision of maternity leave and so on.
Weiner (1985) distinguishes between those who adopt an 'equal opportunities' perspective, that is, equality of access for both boys and girls to
existing educational benefits, and those who are 'anti-sexist', that is,
who concentrate on the development of girl-centred education. An anti-
sexist perspective, through raising the status of feminine culture, would
give more pupils the opportunity to achieve their potential while
developing high levels of self-esteem because a wider range of acceptable
and worthwhile options would be open to them. This would benefit
boys as well as girls, since activities currently denigrated as cissy would
be more acceptable and carry greater currency among both sexes. The
extent to which this is attainable at present given the constraints which
operate outside the school must be questionable. These two perspectives
however defined, identify the nature of, and the solutions to, sexual
divisions in schooling in quite different ways.

In relation to physical education, Leaman and Carrington (1986)
identify a number of possible interpretations of equal opportunity in
which both of the perspectives mentioned above can be seen:

(a) equality of access;
(b) equality of provision;
(c) equality of participation levels;
(d) equal opportunity to realize potential;
(e) equal performance levels.

Some of these have now been considered with specific reference to
the primary school. It should be possible for access and provision to be
offered to both boys and girls although this is not yet always the case.
Equal participation levels are unlikely to be attained even among junior
school pupils unless extra-curricular provision is scrutinized carefully.
Even if opportunities are ostensibly open to boys and girls, many
influences may inhibit girls from taking part. These may range from
overt hostility from the boys to more subtle influences such as lack of
female role models from the staff in schools where the only staff
contributing to extra-curricular physical education are male. Aiming to
reduce inequalities in participation in existing activities does, of course,
imply a particular view of equality and one which would not necessarily
be acceptable to all people. Offering both boys and girls equal opportunity to achieve their potential is a greater challenge.

The remainder of this chapter looks at some questions which the teacher might ask in the interests of both maximizing girls' and boys' opportunities to achieve their potential in physical education and offering girls a positive self-image.

Some Practical Ways Forward

Curriculum Content

There are various aspects of curriculum content which could be considered in the interests of offering activities which are of equal value and relevance to both girls and boys. It has already been suggested that early segregation of boys and girls for games is unwarranted. This may be avoided by offering versions of games which are traditionally played by both sexes such as hockey or tennis. Alternatively both sexes should be taught whatever games are offered. As Leaman (1984) says,

> Even if girls never again play football and boys never afterwards play netball, these is a lot to be said for an absence of specialization in the junior school.

The balance between individual and team games should also be considered bearing in mind that very few girls continue to play team games after they leave school. Similarly the proportions of competitive and cooperative games are worth consideration. Again, competitive sport is heartily disliked by many adolescent girls. This is not to argue against competition or against team games but whether they should dominate the curriculum must be questioned. This is more of a problem for the junior than for the infant school and is often caused by the demands of school teams or of the school football team dictating curriculum practice.

Where this is the case, both boys and girls are disadvantaged if their talents lie in other directions, but the proportion of girls who suffer is greater than that of boys because not only may girls lack talent in these games, but social conditioning ensures that may of them regard such games as trivial and of little interest. This is, of course, very much the case once adolescence is reached. The difficulty with allowing these games to dominate the primary curriculum is not so much that girls lack motivation to participate at this age, but that they will perceive physical education as involving activities which girls grow out of rather than activities which could form the basis of lifelong physical activity. In this context the inclusion of health-related fitness in the physical education curriculum could be one way of encouraging physical activity as part of a healthy lifestyle as well as interesting both sexes in activity.

Extra curricular provision has already been mentioned. It is worth asking how many school teams are run and for whom? Boys? Girls? Both? If both sexes have the opportunity to play in school teams, are their achievements given equal recognition? As already shown, giving formal access to both sexes does not in any way guarantee that both sexes will take advantage of opportunities offered.

The difficulties of providing a curriculum which is balanced in terms of its contribution to the education of both girls and boys should not be underestimated. Too often the pupils themselves are a major source of difficulty.

> It is the boys rather than the girls who make a balanced physical education programme so difficult to implement in schools. The girls are usually quite prepared to try all sorts of new and 'masculine' activities . . . in a way boys have to become men long before girls have to become women. (Leaman, 1984)

The content of the whole curriculum needs to be scrutinized, not simply that of physical education. An example has already been given of how reading schemes can reinforce the stereotype of sport as a masculine domain. Selection of themes for topic work and examples used in mathematics are further examples of curriculum areas which can be used to reinforce or break down stereotypes. In topic work on the Olympic Games, how much attention is given to female athletes and how much to males? Does measurement in mathematics concentrate on the football pitch or the cricket square, or is the netball court also included?

Organization

The illogicality of giving boys the tasks of moving large equipment at an age when girls are likely to be as strong if not stronger than the boys has already been noted. Organization of groups during activity should also be such that both sexes have equal opportunity to work to the best of their ability.

The question of how far the teacher should intervene in encouraging or forcing boys and girls to work together has to be addressed. Merely putting boys and girls together on a mat in the hall or in a group for a practice will not produce interaction between them. As Galton (1980) observed,

> The typical pupil interacts very largely only with pupils of the same sex. When a group contains several pupils of both sexes, not only is the amount of interaction reduced, but interaction between pupils of opposite sex within these groups is only half that between pupils of the same sex.

It may well be more important to attend to matters such as giving equal attention to boys and to girls and giving equal credit to both than to attempt to force social interactions with which the pupils cannot cope. However, it may well be that organizational aspects of the school take some of the blame for the difficulty pupils have in working in mixed groups. If they are accustomed to being greeted by 'Good morning boys and girls' or to sitting with boys in one half of the hall and girls in the other for assemblies, or to lining up in two lines on sex grounds, then it is perhaps not surprising that they find it difficult to work together in mixed sex groups in other situations.

Language

Some aspects of differential use of language have already been mentioned. Praising girls for their appearance and boys for their strength in gymnastics is an obvious example of undesirable practice.

It is not difficult to find examples of all male groups being insulted by having their play described as 'like a bunch of girls' or 'like a load of old women'. Such practice is unlikely to engender respect for female achievement in sport and physical activity. Similarly, it is not easy for girls to see themselves as having a role to play in the sporting arena if the language used persists in suggesting that they are encroaching upon a male preserve, for example, 'Next batsman please', or 'Which of you was the last man in?'

Teaching Methodology

The tendency to give boys more attention than girls has been well documented. Galton (1980) notes this in the classroom. Leaman (1984) points out that, hardly suprisingly, many primary school teachers are nervous about their physical education classes. The result is that, while apparatus is out, they spend much of their time concentrating on avoiding accidents. This frequently means concentrating on the boys whom they perceive to be in greater danger than the more timid girls.

Secondary physical education teachers have also been criticized for concentrating on the most able at the expense of the rest of the class. Whether this occurs in quite the same way in the primary school is not known. However, in the games situation this would work to further the disadvantage of girls who already suffer from comparatively little out-of-school practice compared with the boys.

It is worth noticing who is asked to demonstrate in physical education lessons. Are boys and girls asked equally? This can be an important way of offering role models to both girls and to boys.

Display work also offers an opportunity for showing girls' and women's achievements in sports as well as those of boys and men.

The tendency for boys to dominate the space in the playground has already been mentioned, having been observed by the pupils interviewed. The implications of this are noted by Leaman (1984),

> It is difficult to over-emphasize the significance of the ways in which children occupy their time in the infant and primary school when at play, but it is one of the most potent areas of sex differentiation.

There are implications here both for curriculum work and for school organization. It should be possible to organize playtime in a way which gives girls the opportunity to play ball games if they so wish. However it is clear that many of them would not choose this method of spending their playtimes even if they had the opportunity. The extra practice which boys have had as far as ball skills are concerned should be taken account of when lessons are being planned.

Conclusions

These are just a few examples of aspects of practice which may encourage or discourage sex stereotyping and which may help to ensure that both sexes receive a rather more equal share of the curriculum cake than has sometimes been the case hitherto. Pupils arrive at school already well along the road to socialization into male and female roles. Simply to ignore sex differences whether biologically or socially determined is no answer. Without mutual respect for one another's interests and achievements little progress will be made. The school cannot remove gender inequalities alone but it can be a powerful influence in encouraging girls to achieve their potential and in countering some of the more negative experiences which girls are likely to encounter outside the school.

References

CLARRICOATES, K. (1980) 'The importance of being Ernest . . . Tom . . . Jane. The perception and characterization of gender conformity and gender deviation in primary schools', in DEEM, R. (Ed) *Schooling for Women's Work*, London, Routledge and Kegan Paul.

EVANS, J. (1984) 'Muscle, sweat and showers. Girls' conceptions of physical education and sport: A challenge for research and curriculum reform', *Physical Education Review*, 7, 1.

GALTON, M., SIMON, B. and CROLL, P. (1980) *Inside the Primary Classroom*, London, Routledge and Kegan Paul.

LABBAN, G. (1974) 'Sex roles in reading schemes', in REEDY, S. and WOODLAND, M. (Eds) (1980) *Family, Work and Education,* London, Hodder and Stoughton.

EAMAN, O. (1984) *Sit on the Sidelines and Watch the Boys Play: Sex Differentiation in Physical Education*, London, Longmans.

LEAMAN, O. and CARRINGTON, B. (1986) 'Equal opportunities and physical education' in EVANS, J. (Ed) *Physical Education, Sport and Schooling*, Lewes, Falmer Press.

MAY and RUDDICK (1983) *Sex Stereotyping and the Early Years of Schooling*, Norwich, Centre for Applied Research in Education, University of East Anglia.

SPORTS COUNCIL (1986) *The Next Ten Years*, London, Sports Council.

TALBOT, M. (1986) 'Gender and physical education', *British Journal of Physical Education*.

WEINER, G. (Ed) (1985) *Just a Bunch of Girls*, Milton Keynes, Open University Press.

WILLIAMS, E.A. (1980) 'Intention versus transaction — the junior school physical education curriculum', *Physical Education Review*, 3, 2.

Chapter 10:
Physical Education in a Multicultural Context

Anne Williams

Introduction

Schools which have pupils from ethnic minority groups should ensure that the curriculum offers them stimulus and opportunity for success. They should be helped to enter fully into a British society which recognizes, respects and draws upon their own culture and traditions. The curriculum in those schools which have no pupils from ethnic minority groups should similarly be of a kind which opens the minds of the pupils to other traditions and other ways of viewing the world and which challenges and dispels the ignorance and distrust which breeds prejudice and discrimination. (DES, 1985)

Attempting to address the issue of multicultural education in one brief chapter is to risk serious oversimplification of complex issues. However it would be remiss to omit any reference to such an important aspect of contemporary education. This chapter begins by considering what we mean by multicultural education before examining the contribution of physical education to education for a pluralist society.

It should be noted at the outset that issues about race are inextricably bound up with those concerned with gender and class, and that discussion of one in isolation from the others, carries the danger of creating an artificial separation. Be that as it may, the focus of this chapter is multicultural education, that is, an education appropriate to a democratic, culturally pluralist society. This definition, although itself problematic, illustrates the change in thinking and in policy which has taken place since the early days of racially mixed schools. Assimilation which made no allowance for cultural diversity was replaced by integration which encouraged social cohesion and accepted cultural differences as necessary irritations with which the teacher had to cope and which might require a certain amount of curriculum adaptation. More recently, multicultural education has been based upon an acceptance of the richness which cultural diversity can bring and on the fact that social justice demands the recognition of different cultural values and mores as being resources rather than problems.

All societies are an amalgamation of peoples who have been brought together over time. Changes in social composition are part of any society. The Asian and Afro-Caribbean groups, which are the main focus of this chapter, are two of many groups living in Britain. There are many communities within each of these ethnic groups. It is important that consideration of all groups and communities forms part of education for a pluralist society.

Modgil *et al.* (1986) suggest that multicultural education is permeated by confusion and contradiction. They contend that there is no agreed definition for the term and that the way in which it is implemented depends largely upon the standpoint of the individuals involved. This implementation may therefore be assimilationist, culturally pluralist or anti-racist in approach. To suggest that multicultural education is a homogeneous entity is thus an oversimplification. The reality is that it subsumes a variety of beliefs, policies and practices in educational provision. Modgil *et al.* ask that a compromise be found between utopian and realistic views. Teaching all children about cultural differences for example may reinforce not reduce their sense of distinctiveness. How does the teacher ensure that white children who have held stereotypical images of black people from a very early age do not simply have them reinforced? On the other hand, it has been argued that many Britons are ethnically illiterate and that the ethnocentric nature of much of what is taught in classrooms can only have an adverse effect on both black and white pupils.

Four aspects of multicultural education can be identified for the purpose of providing a context in which physical education can be discussed. The first is the issue of educating for a pluralist society.

If we accept that we are educating for a pluralist society, then multicultural education becomes a feature of every school and not something which is merely the concern of those whose intake is racially mixed. This is not yet the case in Britain — it is easy to find examples of schools in white communities for whom multiculturalism is seen as irrelevant. However it is as well to be wary of oversimplistic suggestions about how to make education multicultural especially in a school that is in an all white community. The educational principle of starting with the child and his/her community and of selecting experiences which are therefore meaningful, does not sit easily alongside a philosophy of designing curricula which move away from the community value consensus. Moreover such moves bring dangers of reinforcing existing stereotypes.

There are, nevertheless, plenty of examples of the curriculum being designed within a largely taken-for-granted set of assumptions which reflect Britain's present social structure and which draw exclusively on Britain's history. Since much prejudice is based on ignorance, fear or both, this cannot be a satisfactory state of affairs.

Linked with the first aspect discussed, that of educating for a pluralist society is the second, that is, the need to work to counter racism and prejudice. The anti-racism issue is a complex one and has been politicized to the point where the child at school seems at times to have disappeared from sight. There is however no lack of evidence of racist behaviour from pupils, parents and teachers. This is not easy to eliminate. Anti-racist policies applied insensitively can do more harm than good and can increase hostility and prejudice rather than diminishing it. What is even more difficult to counter is the institutionalized racism in society which manifests itself in the organization of schools as much as in other areas of life. As Jones and Kimberley point out, schools have a bad record in devising forms of organization and setting levels of expectation which match the aspirations of black students and their parents. The setting up of supplementary schools for children of West Indian and Asian families is testimony to the failure of the British system to live up to the expectations of parents and community. These schools are also evidence of a belief in the value of education.

It is also worth remembering that a policy of educating children to counter racism and prejudice assumes that teachers themselves share a common concern for the inequalities and discrimination which result from racist attitudes. Many would suggest that this is an unrealistic assumption. It is asking teachers to adopt attitudes and values which are 'ahead' of those of society as a whole. Nevertheless without such an attitude, the aims of multicultural education will be unattainable and the ethos of the school will not be conducive to the kind of respect for individuals which is fundamental to the achievement of equal opportunity for all children. A frequent response to changes about provision made for multicultural education is to argue that the school provides a good education and that all children are treated the same. However, treating children the same generally means treating them all like white children and probably like white middle class children. This will inevitably mean that all children's needs are not being equally met. In any case the reality is that children from different cultural backgrounds are all too frequently accorded different treatment. The fact that expectations of children vary according to a range of factors including social background has been extensively researched. The stereotyping of Asians as quiet and hard working and West Indians as lazy and liable to cause trouble is well documented. The same treatment is thus rarely meted out to all children, and if it were, the question of their different needs would not be addressed.

A third aspect of multicultural education does, of course, involve consideration of the interests of all of the ethnic groups present in the school. The provision of books which contain all white images (and generally middle class white) is not conducive to inculcating respect for different cultures in an all white school. The effects are however less immediate than in a school where black children thereby have no role models or self-images. In the context of physical education, a narrowly focused games curriculum may reflect on white middle class culture in contrast to a curriculum which introduces children to a variety of game forms and in so doing offers something with which children from many different cultures can identify.

Finally, consideration of the diversity of ethnic backgrounds which may be present in one school is, of course, part of promoting equal opportunities. It is artificial to separate race from class and gender on this issue. Mention has already been made of the inadequacy of policies of treating all children the same. The interpretations of equality of opportunity which were discussed in relation to gender could also be applied here.

Physical Education in a Multicultural Context

It is very difficult to be sensitive, flexible or sympathetic in attitude without an adequate knowledge base.

Teachers need knowledge and an understanding of the cultural milieux from which the British school population may be drawn, that is, ethnic literacy. This is as important in the context of physical education as in other subject and involves some issues which may be less relevant to other subjects.

Physical activity and play activity are of little importance in some Asian communities and some Asian children may therefore arrive at school having had little opportunity for physical play. This can affect both their ability and their attitude to physical education. Parents may undervalue opportunities for play or consider sport so unimportant compared with academic pursuits that the child's attitude and performance are affected. In such cases, simply treating all children in the class the same will mean that these particular children's needs are unlikely to be met. Positive action will be needed by the teacher to secure the support of the parents and to convince them of the value of the physical education programme offered. This may be easier to achieve at primary than at secondary level, because there tends to be less formality and opportunities to chat informally with parents are frequently greater. However, it will require a conscious effort on the part of the teacher since parents who have not chosen to accept all aspects of Western culture may well be the last to initiate conversation with the teacher. Furthermore, such conversation may be hindered by language difficulties. These are not insuperable problems but they do demand an effort and a commitment on the part of the teacher.

Muslim families holding strong religious beliefs may well be concerned about girls' participation in the mixed physical education classes which are the norm in most junior schools. Restrictions are more marked for older girls, however levels of modesty expected in mixed company are such that some adaptation may be necessary in for example changing arrangements and dress. Both Sikh and Muslim culture demand that women should cover their legs. This requires no more than minor adaptations in schools where it is not common practice to allow the wearing of tracksuits. The area which may cause difficulty is swimming. Girls can arrive at secondary school as non-swimmers because they have not been allowed to join in primary school classes which are usually, of necessity, mixed. In this situation the school has first to persuade the community that swimming is an important life skill and then look for ways of enabling children to learn to swim. If community leaders can be convinced that swimming is important and can influence parents then a compromise may be reached whereby girls are allowed to join in mixed swimming classes. It may be possible to arrange for some community provision outside the school where single sex pool time can be arranged. The key is likely to be relationships with the local community. This issue is one of several where the principle of respecting alternative cultures can conflict with that of equal opportunities for boys and girls.

The wearing of turbans and religious symbols by Sikh boys also demands tact on the part of the teacher. Difficulties over, for example, the removal of the Kara (bangle) for physical education are unlikely provided that communication between school and community is good. If there is a problem then the Kara can be taped over for physical education so that it does not constitute a danger to others or to its wearer.

Understanding of custom and practice in relation to religious festivals is also important. If children are expected to fast at certain times, for example Ramadan, then their capacity to cope with vigorous exercise is likely to be affected. Muslim boys may be expected to go to the Mosque daily. This may affect their opportunity to be involved in after-school activity. The disadvantages suffered by girls whose opportunities for playing outside school are restricted compared with those available to boys has been mentioned in chapter 9. Asian culture may further restrict girls' play activities by expecting them to return home immediately after school to help in the house.

It is important to remember that knowledge of cultural practices should not result in assumptions being made or stereotyping on racial grounds. There is probably as much variation within Asian culture as within 'white' culture. This is due both to the differences between the various Asian communities who have settled in Britain and to variations in the extent to which individual families have been or wish to be 'Westernized'. Education levels are probably more significant determinants of cultural attitudes and attitudes towards physical education than race or religion. The dangers of stereotyping are equally applicable in the case of Afro-Caribbean pupils.

Afro-Caribbean families also have distinctive cultural, linguistic and social traditions. The early failure to recognize the differences between standard English and patois (particularly Creole) or even to accept that patois is a legitimate language form rather than 'lazy' English, led to severe language problems for West Indian children. Academic under-achievement resulted at least in part from these language difficulties. Since many Afro-Caribbean parents have great academic aspirations for their children the disaffection felt by Afro-Caribbean youth is not surprising. The alienation of West Indian youngsters from British education is contrasted sharply with the high profile which education enjoys in Jamaica.

The West Indian family system is more matriarchal in contrast with the patriarchal Asian family. There is often a strong sense of kinship which extends beyond the immediate family and children are frequently expected to help in the home to a greater extent than white children.

Because West Indians were seen as the most Anglicized of the groups coming to Britain, there was an assumption that adaptation and acceptance would be straightforward. However, many apparent similarities are superficial and hide divergences in attitudes and expectations as well as in cultural and social patterns. Caribbean parents have therefore been seeking evidence of aspects of their culture in the curriculum of British educational institutions. So far they have generally been disappointed.

Knowledge is therefore essential, so that children's needs and expectations can be understood. The dangers of stereotyping have already been mentioned. Here physical education finds itself in contrast with much of the curriculum. While much attention has rightly been given to underachievement of Afro-Caribbean pupils in academic areas, there is plenty of evidence which points to the overrepresentation of black pupils in school teams. For much black youth, male and female, positive role models are easier to find in the sporting arena than elsewhere. The image of black success in sport, combined with the evidence of underachievement in the academic curriculum, leads teachers to expect success in physical activities but poor performance in other curriculum areas. Black pupils thus succeed in physical education but at the expense of success in those academic activities which provide a means to success as adults in the employment market. There is thus a danger that, from the moment the black child enters school, he or she will only achieve in the physical domain. Black parents are deeply suspicious of the channelling of children into physical rather than academic activity which can happen in the secondary school as a means of coping with disaffected youngsters. There are, therefore, likely to be equally suspicious of any suggestion that the primary school teacher has similar expectations. The reality, of course, is that the range of physical abilities within one race is far greater than that between races and that there is no conclusive evidence to suggest that, in general terms, one race is physically superior or inferior to another. Different body types are an advantage in different sports. Children who are physically mature will be at an advantage in physical education throughout their years at primary school. For this reason evidence of progress is of far greater significance than absolute measures of performance.

It is, therefore, important for the primary school teacher to use the role models which are readily available from sport to help both black and white children to acquire a positive self-image. Rather than devaluing black success in sport, every effort needs to be made to provide positive black role models in other areas of life.

For Asian pupils stereotypes in physical education again differ from those in other curriculum areas. The Asian pupil is typically seen as physically frail, lacking in stamina and likely to underachieve in physical education, in contrast to their stereotype as quiet, hardworking and intelligent in the classroom. Again there is likely to be more variety within the ethnic group than between groups, and a tendency to describe as 'natural', differences which are predominantly cultural. Stereotyping Asian pupils as physically weak is just as likely to become a self-fulfilling prophecy as is the stereotyping of Afro-Caribbeans as academically inferior. Where Asian pupils do quite clearly underachieve in physical education, the content of the curriculum should be questioned. This will be discussed later.

Stereotyping can, therefore, clearly disadvantage all groups within the school. Furthermore, it constitutes a clear example of racism and as such should be countered. Commitment to a philosophy of equal opportunity means satisfying the needs of all children and giving them an equal chance to achieve their potential, whether this be in the academic or the physical fields. In terms of physical education, it demands a reexamination of curriculum content. In the infant school, where children are being introduced to a range of physical activities, it should be reasonably easy to ensure that a variety of activity is offered and one which gives children with a range of background, culture and previous experience the chance to succeed.

In the junior school and particularly with older juniors, the focus of games activities is important. The traditional pattern of boys playing football while girls play netball takes no account of the variety of cultural traditions in sport. The domination of the games curriculum by those games in which the school is likely to produce a team is not in the interests of the majority of pupils. This question of curriculum content is therefore one example of multicultural education equalling good education. Introducing pupils to a range of skills and modified games will involve the inclusion of activities which are relevant to many children including those from a variety of cultures. There is a strong tradition in Asian culture of excellence in cricket and racket games. The Jamaican tradition in cricket is demonstrated annually. Children can therefore identify with those activities far more easily than with, for example, rugby or in the case of Asian pupils with football or netball.

There are many informal games which are played on the Indian sub-continent which could well be included as part of the physical education curriculum. Examples of these can be found in *PE for a Multicultural Society* (Coventry LEA). Moray House in Scotland has produced a *World Sports and Games* pack designed to give a multicultural/anti-racist perspective to primary school projects associated with the 1986 Commonwealth Games held in Edinburgh. It is, therefore, possible to offer a games curriculum with which children from many different cultures can identify and which, in an all white school, offers the opportunity for displays which provide examples of world class players from many different ethnic groups. If, however, the physical education curriculum is games dominated it will not necessarily meet the needs of all pupils.

Gordon (1986) suggests that the dance educator is particularly well-placed to use the richness of the world's cultures to promote multicultural education, while warning of the danger of assuming that all peoples of the world have the same concept of dance. The difficulty here, of course, is that many primary school teachers lack the confidence to teach any dance at all, let alone to try to include a more explicitly multicultural element. Where there are ethnic minority pupils in the school there is the possibility of learning from them. It is possible that traditional dance may be a part of their recreational activity. However, although examples from the local community may be a useful starting point, selection of material should obviously not be restricted to those ethnic groups which happen to be near at hand. There are a number of dance in education groups which will come to school to work with pupils and some of these are concerned with a broad range of ethnic dances. It would be wrong to suggest that using ethnic dance is guaranteed success. Black pupils who see themselves as British may well be insulted by being offered African dance.

Nevertheless even where dance from different nationalities cannot be a part of the day-to-day curriculum, it can be included as part of project work which looks at different cultures.

Curriculum content is, therefore, an important factor in the provision of multicultural education in physical education. Equally important is respect and allowance for the different cultures within a school in matters of dress, procedure and expectation. The unacceptability of stereotyping has been discussed. However knowledge of the different social and child-rearing patterns which may be operating in particular communities can help the teacher to understand why children's performance varies. Attitude to physical education is likely to be affected by parental attitude. If parents see physical education as unimportant and insignificant this can clearly affect the motivation of the child. Asian families, particularly those whose own memories of physical education are of drill may well undervalue physical education. Afro–Caribbean families may wish to play down the importance of physical education for quite different reasons, fearing that their child will be labelled as 'only' good at physical tasks. The teacher's role will be to persuade parents that physical education is valuable and in the case of Afro–Caribbean parents, that the self-esteem which can come from success in physical education can be a positive advantage, helping towards achievement across the curriculum.

The need for flexibility in attitude to matters such as dress and changing arrangements has already been mentioned, as has the importance of involving the local community with the life of the school. Community involvement has to be a key element in the success of a school's policies. The parent/teacher divide remains within many schools. Parents are still seen as a nuisance to be tolerated rather than as a source of help. From the parents' viewpoint, the difficulties of communicating with the teacher are such that someone with an understanding of both the community language and the educational expectations of a particular cultural group is needed if the parents' views about school are to be articulated. Parents who have grown up in a culture where the school enjoyed a status similar to that of the church and had an authority which was not questioned will not approach their childrens' school without considerable encouragement. Prominent members of the community may be well placed to act as catalysts especially in the first instance. The teacher will need to persuade members of the community of the value of physical education. The curriculum leader in the primary school must play an important part here.

As well as influencing the child's attitude to physical education, parental attitude is likely to affect the child's previous experience and therefore his/her competence both on entering and in progressing through school. For some Asian parents, play has little educational significance and children therefore have few toys and spend little time on 'play' activities. Lack of play activity may well result in limitations in motor coordination and physical skill in comparison with children whose opportunities for play have been rich. The child may thus be disadvantaged in physical education through limited previous physical activity experiences. This disadvantage is likely to continue if the child is denied the opportunites of extra-curricular activity or informal play enjoyed by other children. This is not a solely multicultural problem. Girls are disadvantaged compared with boys in the same way. It is important that the teacher recognizes that a child's limitations may well not be physical but may be due simply to lack of opportunity.

So far we have considered how the teacher can try to offer equal opportunities in physical education to children from varying cultural backgrounds and have noted the importance of avoiding racist stereo-types in respect of physical abilities. Physical education should, of course, contribute to the achievement of the aims of education in areas other than the purely physical. A key concern in the primary school is language development, and it is perhaps to this area above all others that physical education should contribute in a multicultural context.

It has been said that physical education is less language dependent than other subject areas and that, therefore, physical education for the bilingual child should not be a problem area. However, all too often the bilingual child who lacks sufficient understanding to follow the teacher's instructions is limited to copying other children. While this may be an acceptable start in that the child is at least able to do something, it is far from satisfactory in the long term. The child underachieves in physical education and a great opportunity for using the physical medium to enhance language development is lost. Daley (1988) gives many prac-tical suggestions of ways in which physical education can support language development. The primary school teacher who is responsible for delivering the whole curriculum to a particular class is well placed for this sort of work. Words used in physical education can be reinforced in the classroom and vice versa. For example work could focus on prepositions such as 'along', 'across', 'over', 'under'. Concepts such as 'large' and 'small' can be developed in physical education and in the classroom. Since children generally have to share equipment space or apparatus, many opportunities arise for communication in a context and for a purpose. As physical skills are repeated so language can be practiced or repeated alongside. The use of resource cards with pictures and words is another invaluable aid.

Physical education can also play a part in supporting bilingualism among children. This means giving recognition and support to the language which children bring to school. Children can use dual text task cards for example.

Many of the points which have been made concern good educational practice and it could be argued that they are not specific to the multicultural situation. We are nevertheless far from a situation where complacency about our success in educating for a pluralist society would be warranted. The point was made early in this chapter that education for a pluralist society is the concern of every school and not simply a matter for those whose intake is racially mixed. This is as relevant to physical education as to other subject areas. The curriculum leader in physical education can play an important part in ensuring that the subject is not omitted from debate and decision-making. Examination of the literature available in this area reveals few, if any, references to physical education, a reflection of ignorance of its potential on the part of headteachers and academics.

References

ARORA, R. and DUNCAN, C. (1986) *Multicultural Education: Towards Good Practice*, London, Routledge and Kegan Paul.

CARRINGTON, B. (1986) 'Sport as a sidetrack: An analysis of West Indian involvement in extra-curricular sport' in COHEN, L. and COHEN, A. (Eds) (1986) *Multicultural Education — A Sourcebook for Teachers*, London, Harper.

CASHMORE, E. and TROYNA, B. (1983) *Introducing Race Relations*, London, Routledge and Kegan Paul.

COHEN, L. and MANION, L. (1983) *Multicultural Classroom*, London, Croom Helm.

COVENTRY LEA (1984) *Physical Education for a Multicultural Society*, Coventry, Elm Bank Teachers Centre.

CRAFT, A. and BARDELL, G. (Eds) (1984) *Curriculum Opportunities in a Multicultural Society*, London, Harper.

DALEY, D. (1988) 'Language development through physical education', *British Journal of Physical Education,* 19, 3.

DES (1985) *Curriculum 5–16,* London, HMSO.

GORDON, D. (1986) 'Multicultural education and the dance educator', *Dance, The Study of Dance and the Place of Dance in Society,* Proceedings of the VIII Commonwealth and International Conference on Sport, Physical Education, Dance, Recreation and Health, London, Spon.

GUNDARA, J., JONES, C. and KIMBERLEY, K. (Eds) (1986) *Racism Diversity and Education,* London, Hodder and Stoughton.

HOULTON, D. (1986) *Cultural Diversity in the Primary School,* London, Batsford.

JEFFCOATE, R. (1984) *Ethnic Minorities and Education,* London, Harper and Row.

LYNCH, J. (1986) *Multicultural Education: Principles and Practice,* London, Routledge and Kegan Paul.

MODGIL, S., VERMA, G., MALLICK, K. and MODGIL, C. (Eds) (1986) *Multicultural Education: The Interminable Debate,* Lewes, Falmer Press.

TIERNEY, J. (Ed) (1982) *Race Migration and Schooling,* London, Holt, Rinehart and Wilson.

TWITCHIN, J. and DEMUTH, C. (1985) *Multicultural Education,* London, BBC.

VASSEN, T. (1986) 'Curriculum considerations in the primary school' in GUNDARA, J., JONES, C. and KIMBERLEY, K. (Eds) *Racism Diversity and Education.*

VERMA, G. (1986) *Ethnicity and Educational Achievement in British Schools,* London, Macmillan.

Notes on Contributors

Alan Asquith is a Principal Lecturer at Westminster College, Oxford.

Grant Biddle is a Teacher/Adviser for Physical Education with Kent County Council.

Stuart Biddle is a Lecturer in the School of Education, University of Exeter.

Rosie Connell is Head of Studies in Physical Education and Recreation, Trinity and All Saints College, Leeds.

Lilian Groves is Vice Principal of St. Hilda's College, Durham.

Chris Rose is a Physical Education Adviser with Devon County Council.

Craig Sharp is Chief Physiologist to the British Olympic Medical Centre and a Lecturer in Sports and Exercise Sciences, University of Birmingham.

Anne Williams is a Lecturer in Physical Education and Senior Tutor to the Postgraduate Certificate in Education course, University of Birmingham.

Index

Index

Index